Over Early Saxon Fields

5th and 6th Century
Surrey and Beyond

C. Howkins

Chris Howkins

Published by
Chris Howkins

ISBN 978-1-901087-90-1

PUBLISHER
Chris Howkins,
70 Grange Road,
New Haw,
Addlestone,
Surrey,
KT15 3RH

PRINTED
Hobbs the Printers Ltd.
Brunel Road,
Southampton,
Hampshire,
SO40 3WX

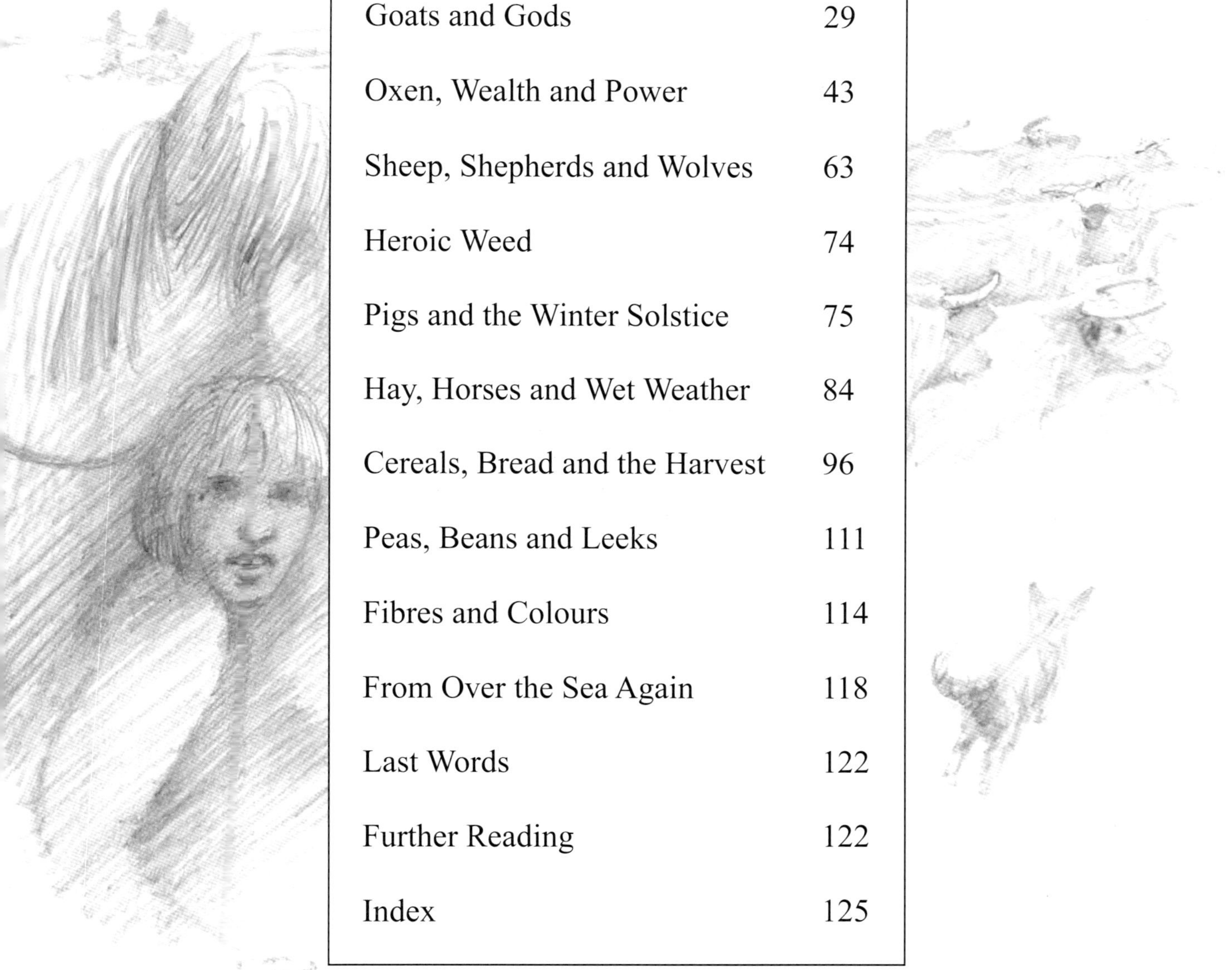

CONTENTS

INTRODUCTION

This book explores the look of the land in Early Saxon England, trying to give impressions by word and image of what would be seen by anybody walking across the fields. It is such a vast subject that the emphasis has indeed been kept upon the fields, rather than the overall landscape. There are only limited references to the trees, woodlands and coppices as managed resources in the countryside, while the homes and settlements have been omitted altogether as they deserve a volume in their own right. Similarly, the text has been curtailed at the point where produce from the fields went off for processing, with the exception of grinding corn, which was too important to ignore.

The traditional story of the founding of Anglo-Saxon England is well established and founded primarily upon the writings of Gildas and Bede. Anything that archaeologists unearthed has been slotted into their story lines until in recent years a few bold archaeologists started insisting that we let the archaeology speak for itself. That has caused the rewriting of the story of the period, which has in turn stirred debate and fierce arguments since so much depends upon interpretation. It all makes for good reading but the writers rarely give much attention to the overall farming landscape in which to imagine the people living and working. There is a lot of information available so when a lecturer answered a question with, "Oh, we have no idea what early Saxon Surrey looked like," I was not inclined to concur and started thinking about this present volume.

Admittedly there are still thousands of unanswered questions but there are also thousands for which there *are* now answers, even if they are still debated or disputed. We will only learn and understand by a healthy debate of ideas and interpretations. Consequently this book contains a whole ship-load of such words as 'maybe', 'perhaps', and 'possibly', for which no apology is made. We need to explore further for certainties and when suggestions stir debate so much the better.

My prime interest is in the people and so on a walk across the fields my attention would be caught by those at work—who were they, what were their beliefs, what were their standards, values, hopes and fears etc.? These aspects have been worked into the text where appropriate but of course this book is like their plough —it only scratches the surface.

TIME AND NAMES

The time span chosen covers the 5th and 6th centuries, from the time the Roman legions departed to the arrival of St. Augustine in 597. Within this span there is a bias towards the early years because I was interested particularly in the developments and new ideas that enable this period used to be called the 'Dark Ages' due to the lack of documentary evidence but it is not nearly so dark as previously, thanks to the skills of modern archaeologists and the advanced sciences available to them. Consequently, new names have come into use, with the Saxon period being divided into the three phases of Early, Mid and Late, with the former Dark Ages being the Early. The term 'Early Saxons' has

Anyone going to the viewpoint on Epsom Downs by the Grandstand can gaze northwards over the Thames Valley, as sketched above. It spreads out as an expansive landscape that disappears into the haze in the north. With London being the most polluted capital in Europe it is rare now to see as far as the line of blue hills that marks the far side of the Thames Valley. Beside the trees on the far right above is a glimpse over to the tower blocks of the City of London, although that portion of the view is becoming obscured rapidly with tall trees. Trying to locate other places is difficult because they too are obscured by millions of trees when viewed from this angle but this might be close to the appearance viewed by the Romans since they must have maintained many coppices for fuel. Not only was firewood needed for all the cooking fires but also for industrial processing and some of those would have needed charcoal, which was also a coppice product. Otherwise the wooded landscape was interspersed with small square fields, for this was predominantly a farming landscape. There were many squares of cereal crops, from wheat and barley to oats and rye. More squares provided beans and there were probably some for peas. Somewhere among all these was land used for industrial plants, from flax for linen to woad for blue dye. Small portions of land grew leeks, onions and other pot herbs. Presumably the herbalists grew some of their medicinal plants that were not otherwise available locally. There was lots of grassland too, for pasturing the sheep, goats and cattle needed for daily supplies of dairy produce and fresh meat. The Romans had this valley highly productive, up to their town of Staines and beyond. This was a good place to be and it was into this landscape that the Early Saxons arrived. Settlements took on a Saxon identity right up the Thames, with Dorchester-on-Thames becoming influential at an early date, especially for Christianity. From there, evangelists were sent out to convert some of the pagans of Surrey, as the Early Saxon period merged into the Mid Saxon period.

been used in this volume but that raises a problem. It implies that the people to be seen across the fields were all immigrant 'Saxons' from over the North Sea whereas in reality there was a cultural mix. There were foreigners left-over from the Roman occupation and they could have originated anywhere in the Empire. There were the descendants of the original native stock, still following many of the old Iron Age ways, albeit updated under Roman influence and the general influence of 'progress' over 400 years. Therefore it must be stressed that in this book 'Early Saxon' refers to the time period rather than to ethnic origins. In many cases it refers to new ideas and styles and new ways of doing things but even if those came from over the North Sea it does not mean that they were brought here by a 'Saxon'. Indeed they may have been introduced at the end of the Roman period and taken time to establish themselves out in the countryside.

Other name changes have occurred. That initial phase of cultural mix is usually called the Romano-British period but is now often called sub-Roman which has not been used in this book since it omits the reminder that the descendants of the Iron Age British lived through the Roman period into Saxon times. It also sounds rather negative and inferior. It was, in the eyes of all those writers who had a classical education that cast the Romans in a golden light of civilisation, and described everybody else as 'barbarians'. Another popular notion has been 'the migration period' but the paucity of archaeological evidence in support of mass migration to England from the Continent makes this unsound. Just as unsound is calling it the 'pagan period' since we know now that Christianity did not sail down the Thames

with the departing legions, as was once thought. It lived on and is now believed to have been more common and more influential than was guessed even a few years ago. It is now being suggested, in some instances at least, that the Christian Church took over some of the administration from the Romans. Nevertheless there were plenty of pagans around in those centuries and it is that social group upon which this book concentrates and has been cast from a pagan viewpoint. The rising power of the Church carries the story into the 'mid-Saxon' period which is beyond the present remit.

PEOPLE AND IDEAS

The starting point has been that there were people working the landscape in the period. How they came to be there, whether by birth or by immigration, is not explored. Traditionally the Saxons were immigrants by conquest but modern archaeology is not providing evidence of conquest. Instead it is revealing a story of continuity as though any immigrants were assimilated into the social structure peacefully. It looks as though it was the influx of new ideas that changed society so decidedly. Therefore the text is slanted more towards acculturation. Apart from the evidence, it makes theoretical sense since there must surely have been a mixture of peoples with their own differing ideas working together in the Thames valley to service the needs of such a cosmopolitan city as London. It is not surprising that we find evidence for this in the valley. The same presumption would lead us to expect that the further south in Surrey we look the more likely we are to find native Romano-British evidence than Continental Saxon and again that is to a large extent fulfilled. That said, it is often very difficult to determine Romano-British from Saxon. Perhaps such distinctions were not even clear-cut at the time. Think of our own times and the influx of Continental immigrants, arriving in London and spreading out wherever they think there are good opportunities, such as working in the vegetable fields. There may be several nationalities picking greens but they are all trying to make a fresh start, all learning a new language, all learning to fit in, no matter where they came from. It is at home that most of the ethnic differences prevail. It does not seem far removed from the fields reviewed in this book.

Therefore, to stress the point, the people in this book described as 'Early Saxon' should be taken to mean 'the people of the time' rather than a specific ethnic group.

That said, the selection of information to work from has been gathered where possible, or where known, from that designated as Saxon, rather than Anglian, Jutish, Frankish or whatever. In terms of the agricultural landscape they all seem to have being doing the same and so differences in ethnic origins are probably not crucial. Material has been used from the excavated 'Saxon' village at West Stow, even though the people ought, theoretically, to have been Angles. West Stow is a major source of information for the period and the site (near Bury St. Edmunds) is well worth a visit. From the excavated ground plans of the habitations they have rebuilt a range of superstructures according to the different possibilities. There are museum displays of the actual finds plus reconstructions ranging from an ard to the costume. Each year they have re-enactment days too – see website for programme, www.stedmundsbury.gov.uk/sebc/play/weststow-asv.cfm.

Although material that was not specific to the Saxons has been avoided, it has been only a general principle. Difficulties arise along the borders; Kent has traditionally been peopled by Jutes and Surrey by Saxons but what about blending along the border? Then there is the problem that East and West Kent are revealing distinctions with more 'Jutish' material in East Kent and the later records show the kingdom was divided. It all made a difference when it came to the illustrations; what design of brooch should I pin the women's dress with? One design was not used apparently in Surrey but then I discovered one had been found! I avoided the problem and drew no close-up! Also missing are the things called 'girdle hangers' by archaeologists because again I'm told one has not been found in Surrey and if these attachments to women's belts were indeed to send out social messages then my drawings should have whatever was their equivalent in Saxon lands. Costume was a major problem in the book production and as you will see, it has been simplified right down. Fortunately Penelope Walton Rogers' appraisal of the evidence to date was published before I had finished and some fresh drawings could be made. I've used the simplest design of headdress because I needed farmwear and probably low status too, since many of the workers were slaves. I did consider the wrap-around style (*illus. below*) but decided that was best suited for winter use since it covered the throat like a scarf but the women in my fields are all slogging away in the summer. The same text has men's footwear as rather elaborate with decorative piercing etc. which did not seem well suited to farm work so I've drawn a pull-on boot with soft leather that sags round the ankle because that would be more serviceable and crucially that is what was unearthed in Surrey by Steve Poulton.

Example of wrap-around headdress, thrown back over shoulder to reveal one of the pair of shoulder brooches that fixed the dress front. It is surmised that she released one of these to facilitate breast feeding.

THE ILLUSTRATIONS

It was decided from the outset not to give much space to the landscape itself because the bones of the hills and valleys are there to seen today, just as are heathlands and pastures. Emphasis was to be upon subjects within the landscape, concentrating upon differences and highlighting those birds, flowers and animals to which we know the Saxons paid attention.

The intention was to include lots of people and all the figures and faces have been drawn from life (sometimes with photographic help). Most were happy to lose a few pounds of weight but changes in hairstyle and costume did not always meet with approval! No attempt has been made to get a specifically 'Saxon' look because genetic research into that has not been completed but offers from a couple with a distinctly Irish look were declined (amicably!). Reducing people's weight met with approval but not to the point of emaciation (!) so all the people (and animals) look well fed but Saxons did have good years as well as famine years.

Costume was kept very generalised and simple, based on notes made at the reconstructed Saxon village at West Stow, and with reference to the plates in Glasswell (who acknowledges Leicester City Museums Service). Then, halfway through the project, Rogers was published, necessitating some adjustments. Written evidence was taken into account from archaeology reports to narrow down more carefully what was probably on view in Surrey.

Ultimately the illustrations chosen have been the same mixture of landscapes, figure studies, portraits and working details as I would produce on any field trip into today's landscapes. Even that has kept the office shredder very busy! Very frustrating has been the way the text moves from topic to topic so quickly that there has been the option of using but one or two illustrations alongside; very frustrating when a day at the sheep-shearing resulted in over twenty studies! Unless stated otherwise the drawings relate to the text on that page, to avoid a litter of captions, and where a comment might be of value it has been added after the end-notes.

BACKGROUND

Of all the peoples and periods I have looked into and written about since the 1960s none has caught my imagination more than the Saxons. They were the first too. I was a young teenager, with no interest in such things, who thought history was vaguely anything pre-granny, until I was walked down through the Devil's Punch Bowl to Thursley and into the church. I was stood in the chancel and my gaze directed through the deep splays of the two little Saxon windows in the north wall *(illus. right)* and told to imagine I was the Saxon priest doing just that a thousand years before. A thousand years! My imagination was on the move. The wooden window frames were Saxon too and inspired talk about the craftsman who fashioned them and saw them inserted to his satisfaction. Our next walk was to the south, over Blackdown, to find the source of the River Wey at Cotchet Farm *(illus. left)*. The odd name I was told was Saxon and referred to a sheep fold, that this was where they had brought the ewes at lambing time, sheltered in the valley, with water always to hand, and the wolves howling on Blackdown. I thought the wolves were a bit over the top but now I know that was a real possibility.

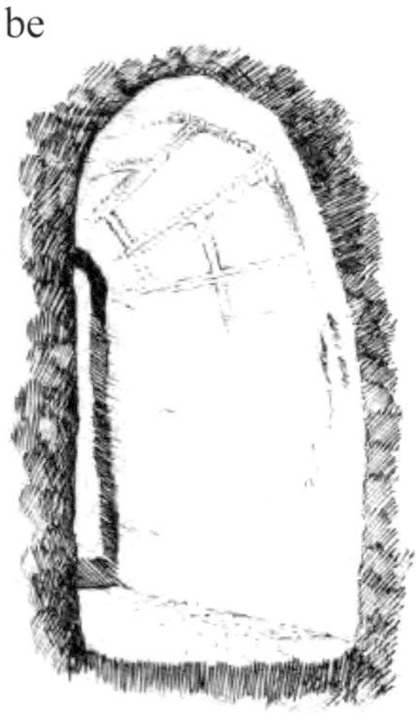

The rest of the summer became weekly trips to Saxon churches : Stoke D'Abernon, Worth, Sompting, Corhampton, Bosham, Singleton; anywhere that could be reached by bus and train. I signed up for an archaeology course and was soon pot-washing at Fishbourne Roman Palace and digging for Roman soldiers outside East Walls at Chichester – where the soil flashed green as my trowel scraped the bronze ankle bracelet of my first skeleton.

The Saxon carpenter who crafted the window frames did so from an oaken plank for a Christian church in a village named after a pagan god whose sacred tree was the oak. That inspired a life-long interest in the relationship between people and the plants around them. It was over twenty years later when the curator of Weybridge Museum produced a Saxon pot for me to draw *(illus. left)*. There it sat in a nest of tissue in its cardboard box. "Lift it out," she said, and as I did so I realised there were 'hand-holds' for doing just that – but I couldn't see them. Tilting it to the light showed nothing but under my finger tips I could feel them. I'd put my fingers into the very places where the potter had last put his when lifting the wet pot and in so doing had compressed the clay ever so slightly. To change places with a Saxon potter was as inspiring as the oak frames smoothed by the carpenter. Saxons slipped in and out of my ethnobotany work over the years until I put together *Oak: The Lightning Tree* and went to the lecture that started this volume.

WHOSE LAND WAS IT ?

In order to set the scene, let us go back to a date shortly after 410 CE when the Roman legions were withdrawn,[1] leaving the people of Britannia to fend for themselves. Imagine an adventurer from Frisia (northern Netherlands today) who had taken employment upon a trading ship that had survived the notorious crossing of what the Frisians called the North Sea. The crossing had been very rough, for it was nearing the end of the shipping season and all would be laid up soon for the winter, so he thanked his gods when land came into sight. The waters narrowed into the estuary of the *Tamesis* and they rode the rising tide that was forcing flocks of estuarine birds to swirl above the ship. The Frisian squinted into the setting sun for his first sight of *Londinium* that the Romans had developed into a trading port of significance. On either side he could see the rising smoke from the cooking fires in the settlements, for it was approaching the time of day to eat and he realised his hunger, for they did not carry rations on board. The *Tamesis* was narrowing all the time and soon he would be staring in wonder at the great stone wall of *Londinium* on the northern bank, foreign to the Frisian who came from a culture that built in timber, not stone. He ran his eye over the long timber wharves in front and saw that they were good. Soon he would be standing on them. Better still, he would be breaking his bread at an eating house.

Had he asked a local whose land it was he could have heard that the Romans had administered through the tribal entities of the native people and therefore as the trader's ship had sailed into the estuary of the *Tamesis* the land to the south belonged to the *Cantiaci* centred upon *Durovernum Cantiacorum* (Canterbury).[2] As the ship approached *Londinium* that southern shore became the territory of the Atrebates, which extended up the valley of the *Tamesis* and was centred upon *Calleva Atrebatum* (Silchester).[3] When the trader had turned to view the northern shore he was looking at the land of the Trinovantes, centred upon Colchester.[4] At *Londinium*, however, the trader was sitting in the territory of the Catuvellauni who had their capital at *Verulamiun* (St. Albans) to the north.[5] Perhaps the trader would detect apprehension, for without the Romans enforcing stability, there was fear of power struggles between these peoples. The pride of owning their own land was but a folk memory recited through four hundred years of Roman occupation.

Londinium, to the Frisian, was a wondrous place. It was so big. There were thousands of people, he was told, and it was laid out in streets whereas his village back home was a scattering of homesteads where they passed in all directions from neighbour to neighbour. His own home was of timber and thatch but in *Londinium* there was so much brick and stone and tile, cold and textured as he slid his palm over the wall. He found the market an amazement of foreign wares amid the disconcertion of strange languages, costumes, manners, and symbols of different faiths.

There was a lot to take in for a lad from a farming background. Beyond the city walls the farmers were largely of native stock, working the land, in traditional ways, much as he had done himself. Even here his eye would pause on Roman innovations. The farmers had expectations of doing better, following the departure of the legions, since they would not lose so much of their return to the Roman tax system but that idea was short-lived. The administration still needed funding and people

still expected to be defended so there was also the militia to consider. Administration and defence had been key areas into which the Romans absorbed 'outsiders'. The Romans preferred to be overseers, doing well for doing little, and retreating to their great country estates where villa life was good (Surrey had at least thirteen, probably sixteen, with the possibility of finding more[6]). They trained up astute locals to carry out their orders in their absence. They had no wish to give up that life-style and leave with the legions and so villa life continued (not petering out until about 450). Similarly, the military are believed to have recruited mercenaries to help guard the river approaches, leaving cemeteries of soldiers on the higher ground around London. These are believed to include 'Saxons' although if dressed and equipped in the Roman manner it is very difficult to distinguish Saxon from Roman. Certainly the hilltops provided good views of the river, as for example the famous view from Greenwich. The main fear was of Saxon pirates, since the people of N.W. Europe were a restless lot and had been causing problems on the high seas for quite some time.[7] Setting Saxon against Saxon does not sound good military strategy but the Romans had the sense to allot a land-holding to recruits. That gave them a vested interest while at the same time the tending of crops and livestock deterred them from wandering off.

All in all, our imaginary Frisian could have encountered quite a lot of people from his homelands and probably hear somebody muttering that there were a lot more now than there ever used to be. Some were achieving a permanent place in the land and doubtless sending news of their success back home, so that relatives started to come over to join them. These were not the faint-hearted. Even the sea-faring families had dire tales of the treacherous North Sea so it must have been with some trepidation that they boarded the ships. They sailed round the coastline for about three days, depending on their starting point, and then on about the fourth day they left sight of land behind and headed west across the high seas.[8]

It is at this point in particular that modern archaeological evidence is contradicting the traditional story, which had thousands of migrants making this journey in a sword-thrust conquest of England, in what was dubbed the 'migration period'. Today's evidence does not reveal a Saxon conquest by force. When Boudicca had revolted against the Romans there was a resulting layer of charcoal in the archaeology from where she burned down *Londinium* but there is no charcoal layer from Early Saxon times. Out in the countryside, excavated farms do not have a destruction layer either but tell of continuity. No massed burials with sword-slashed bones have been found or great burial mounds or even place-names recording notable battles. Again and again the evidence tells of continuity, as though the Saxons were absorbed into the landscape with minimum strife. That process has become known as 'acculturation'. It is far less valiant than later Saxon writers would record as the beginnings of Saxon England but because it is based upon archaeological evidence it has steadily gained acceptance, leaving fewer and fewer archaeologists believing in mass migration conquest.

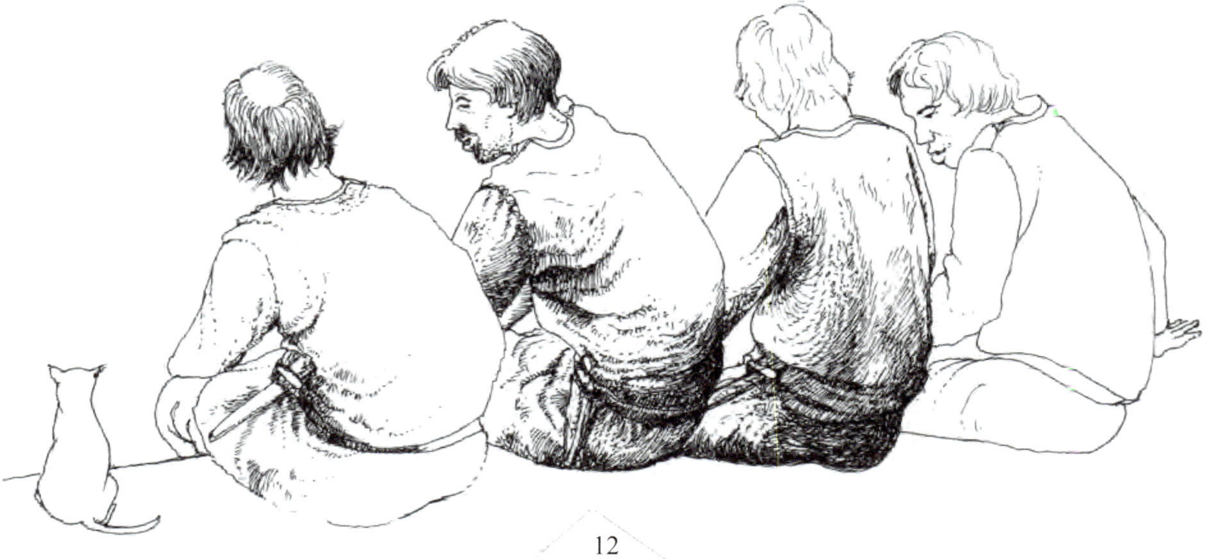

Certainly we can imagine that some migrants gained a permanent place here by finding work out on the farms or by leasing land or by obtaining it through marriage. Some proponents of the acculturation theory make it all sound very peaceful and lovely, which is probably going too far. It is notoriously difficult for archaeologists to find the new settlements because they were built of organic materials that have rotted away but ten have been excavated to date and show a preference for unoccupied hilltops away from the surrounding locals. Should that be interpreted as lack of peace and harmony between the peoples, or is the sample too tiny from which to draw conclusions?

Much more telling is the language. If the Saxons established themselves gradually through acculturation how was the native language wiped out so thoroughly as to leave fewer than twenty Brithonic words in use? If the cultures merged gradually there should be more. The speed with which the Saxon languages became that of England is astonishing. It has led to various calculations as to how long it ought to have taken, with results invariably offering a timescale that sounds too long. That lends weight to the conquest theories but it does not need to have taken long at all. Travellers to foreign countries today, who do not speak the language, are forced to learn the nouns of shopping straight away. They learn the money too which entails counting, measurements and wariness against being exploited. It is a crash course in acculturation. The earliest Saxon traders to *Londinium* could have been highly influential in establishing their language, simply because people wishing to deal with them had to speak their language.

Saxon traders could have established themselves quickly if they cornered the market in desirable commodities, undercut the opposition and paid higher wholesale prices. That of course could have upset the other traders, leading to the Saxons having to guard their assets at night, even if only as a precaution. That would lead to them grouping together and thereby organising themselves as a small separate community. Is that what happened at *Londinium*? Is that why archaeologists found the Early Saxon settlement of *Lundenwic* outside the Roman city walls, a bit to the west, on a strand of gravel that carries 'The Strand' today? Did that site give them the advantage of being outside the jurisdiction of the controlling party of the old city, which some people are now beginning to think could well have been the Christian Church?

Certainly the Church adopted the term 'diocese', which the Romans had used for a political administrative unit, and Christians had been so significantly numerous in *Londinium* as to have totalled a long list of bishops through the Roman period, according to the writings of Jocelyne of Furness. We cannot trust him entirely because he was not writing till Norman times and he is the sole source of the early names, which cannot therefore be cross-checked for accuracy. Going down his list we reach the name Restitutus and he definitely lived, so he is the man accepted by St.Paul's Cathedral as the first bishop of London.[9] He was of sufficient significance to have attended the Council of Arles in 314.[10] The extent of the London diocese of Restitutus and his immediate successors is not known but some argue that it included the 'Surrey' side of the river for the name derives from the Saxon *Sudergeona* or southern region. It could mean, therefore, the southern portion of the diocese of London. We do not know for certain and so we do not know its geographical extent. There is some evidence to suggest that 'Surrey' extended eastwards, either as far as the Medway or the Darent.[11] If all this were so, it would mean that the pagans being explored through the pages of this book lived among far more Christians than was believed by writers even twenty years ago, who were seeing it as a political territory.

If the name *Sudergeona* did refer to a political territory, then whose land was it? The name does not get written down until 672-4 and so there are some 250 years of political turmoil to unravel, without the benefit of many written documents. Obviously the name must have been from a northern viewpoint and therefore likely to be that of 'Londoners'. They became known as the East Saxons (hence Essex) with their territory ranging from the North Sea coast right through present London until it abutted lands of the Angles or Mercians. That raises vexed questions over the

Middle Saxons of Middlesex who ought to be in-between. They are not present in the earliest records but appear suddenly and then disappear again. It has been thought to be a Mercian name and is explained as Mercia annexing this part of the East Saxon kingdom (but others conclude it derives from the viewpoint of Kent, which makes sense). These Angles were a powerful lot. After all, Angle-land became England. Their great expansionist king was Wulfhere and Surrey did not escape his eye. At that time, probably 669, Surrey was held by the Jutes of Kent and this conquest got recorded in a charter of Chertsey Abbey of 672. It appears to confirm the tradition that the abbey had been founded in 666, because it says it '*was first constructed under King Egbert.*'[12] He was king of Kent that year, having succeeded his father two years earlier and was still alive when the charter was written. However, he had obviously lost control over Surrey (probably in 669) because the charter records lands being given not by Egbert of Kent but by Frithwold, a sub-king of Mercia. In due course Mercia would lose all its lands to the West Saxons of Wessex and it was that royal house that eventually united all the Saxon kingdoms as one *Anglelond* or England, and later defended it as such at the Battle of Hastings.

END NOTES

1 That's the accepted date but the evidence is not conclusive.

2 The Cantiaci or Cantii gave their name to Kent/Canterbury.

3 The territory of the Atrebates had been divided into three by the Romans and so this 'Surrey' portion belonged to the Regni (centred upon *Noviomagus Regnorum*/Chichester). It is thought, from the size of the kingdom, that the Atrebates constituted a confederation of lesser tribes and it was the differences between these that were exploited by the Romans when creating more manageable units. The Atrebates were pro-Roman and allowed the Romans to use Chichester harbour. See history of Fishbourne Roman Palace to explore this further.

4 The Trinovantes were particularly powerful which is why the Romans established their first base at Colchester.

5 The Catuvellauni were the most powerful of all so the Romans established Verulamium as one of their first civitae; their name probably meant 'foremost in battle'.

6 Map of them p.9 in *The Roman Temple: Wanborough* from the Surrey Archaeological Society. Tantalisingly, from nowhere in Britain has it been possible to put an owner's name to such a site, so although we call them 'Roman' we don't know whether any British people had risen to this status. To presume all the British remained subservient may be insolent.

7 See Haywood for the overall picture.

8 Some ships had sail while others were rowed. For a full discussion and review of the archaeological evidence see Haywood.

9 The site of his cathedral is unknown; it does not have to be under the present St. Paul's Cathedral.

10 The Council of Arles was the first time that Christians appealed to a secular power for judgement (to Emperor Constantine, against a decision of the Roman council), so Restitutus was involved in formulating early Church law.

11 A theory included by Gavin Smith in *Surrey Place-names*.

12 See Poulton 1988.

MEET THE PEOPLE

MENFOLK

Most readers will need to put aside their images of Saxons because they derive from film and television, which perpetuate their own myths. They are not accurate. Forget dejected, snivelling peasants in tatty brown tunics, with long matted hair. The Early Saxons were dignified. They were largely self-determining in a structured society with high personal and social standards. They walked out with their heads held high.

To elaborate upon that, meet imaginary Ælfred in the drawing. He was winter cheery after a horn of hot elderberry wine. That always cheered him up and being anti-viral helped to keep him in good health. His arthritic joints complained of a long labouring life in the fields, which he still supervised. The elderly were respected and his opinion on the season's progress was always sought. On this day he'd wrapped himself in his wolfskin and been out a bit further to cut his own spray of holly ready for crowning the midwinter king at the great solstice rituals; not to be missed for anything. The promise of new life with the rebirth of the sun reminded him of starting his own new life after braving the waves to England in search of better prospects. He had decided then and there that a life on the seas was not for him. Not that he admitted that at the great feast in the big hall afterwards. Oh no, with a horn of mead inside him his story stretched with valour. His grandson rhythmed along on the harp and his granddaughters sang the chorus lines, while his wife, as hostess, passed among the gathered with the mead.

Such nights bonded the community together and taught youngsters the story of their people. Even though they did not produce written documents until the next phase, the Mid Saxon period, we know a lot about these people because the earliest written documents included law codes. These put into writing what was accepted already, what had become

customary. We know that society was based upon 'the family' and that concept included all related families to create the Early Saxon tribes. Leadership was in the hands of the head man. Although it was male dominated it was possible for a woman to take over the reins.

The tribes are impossible to name without documents and where names occur in those from other cultures they only tell us what those other cultures called the people. It looks as though the Saxons thought of themselves in terms of the name of their leader and that gave rise to some of the Surrey place-names.[1] These personal names would have been of the local landowner and therefore men of status but among them are a few that we can guess were particularly powerful because their landholdings became cultural centres, such as *Wocc* of Woking and *Godhelm* of Godalming. Collectively, these names become particularly interesting in relation to the interpretation of acculturation since it means that Saxons took over local dominance very fast and very thoroughly, since only one Romano-British man left his name as a legacy and he was *Cerot* after whom Chertsey was named. Mention ought to be made of the much-debated name of Leatherhead which many believe to be pre-Saxon in origin but for which there is no documentary evidence until the 9th century by which time it had been corrupted from the original into *Leodridan.* That is probably from the Saxon *leod* for 'people' and reflects its importance as a cultural centre.

Stories of the foundation of the local communities were the stuff of those story-telling nights in the Saxon halls. They gave the people their sense of who they were. Doubtless they were exaggerated for entertainment value and distorted to emphasise cultural values but these proved vital in the creation of a new coherent society in England.

Some would say that the drawing of Ælfred is of a rarity, that only about five out of every hundred men celebrated more than forty midwinter festivals. However, that 5% should be treated with caution since determining age from a skeleton is imprecise and when practitioners were tested with skeletons of a known age they were found to err at either end of the scale. Literature, such as *Beowulf,* looks back on earlier times and is well peopled with seasoned warriors. Ælfred has been drawn freshly shaved, while there was still daylight, ready for the holy day but how frequently men shaved is uncertain. Unearthing a Saxon razor is a great rarity but so is finding a Roman one despite plenty of evidence for shaving. It looks as though beards and moustaches (both drooping and upturned styles) did not become fashionable until the next phase but even then we do not know whether they were visual signals indicating social class, marriage status, allegiance to a specific religious cult, or whatever. We could argue that the thunder god was visualised with a massive beard and so his followers grew the same but equally arguable is the possibility that to imitate the god in this way was impertinent, or, that beards were reserved for the priests. It is difficult to imagine that farm labourers bothered to shave every day but we need to stick to evidence and there isn't any.

We know more about hairstyles. Combs are common among grave goods of both genders and all ages, so obviously they did not have cropped hair. The combs suggest that hair-care and personal appearance were of concern and certainly, in terms of grave goods, it was important that they went off to the Otherworld looking presentable and equipped to stay that way. The combs were beautifully made, of antler, bone or metals (and presumably wood, that has rotted away), and often carved decoratively, which suggests they were valued. It raises the likelihood that even the plain combs were once beautifully painted or stained. The closeness of the teeth ensured the removal of head lice and nits so we should not imagine our Saxons busy scratching; that's the stuff of television and film. Head lice prefer short hair anyway and the evidence tells us that hair was jaw-length. Lice also prefer clean hair but we know nothing of hair-washing except that the herbals contain no recipes for shampoo. That is not significant because the herbals record medicines rather than cosmetics. To leave the natural oils in the hair would help waterproof it for rainy days and stop it blowing in the face so much on windy days. Naturally oily hair is considered beautiful, not dirty, in some cultures today and that might have been the case with the Saxons.

General bodily cleanliness was probably important. Back in the 1st century the Roman writer Tacitus recorded that these people in their homeland took baths but we do not know whether that practice survived 400 years and got brought to Britain. Possibly it did since decline in personal hygiene is usually associated with a fall in self-esteem and self-confidence, which does not sound like the peoples who pioneered settlement in England and created new kingdoms. Furthermore, the herbals instruct adding herbs to the bath water as though that would be understood without further direction. It looks as though the jaw-length hair covered the ears because ear jewellery is surprisingly uncommon, as though the ears were normally hidden. That makes sense when several writers repeat the notion that warriors cut their hair back from their faces *(Illus. far right)* to make them look larger and more intimidating. Such statements probably derive from Tacitus and therefore could be out of date but if true then it would suggest that warriors shaved ahead of conflict and also combed the rest of the hair back from their faces. Normally, hair had a centre parting and fell naturally to the sides and front. An image of head and shoulders would not look out of place today.

Clothing was primarily of wool and linen, with a simple tunic belted at the waist and reaching almost to the knees. Men carried a sheathed knife on their belt and sometimes a bag or purse (possibly an early 'tinder-box'). Leather was used for belts, scabbards and shoes etc. but how often leather or furs were used for clothing is not clear (Penelope Walton Rogers does not include either in her great costume survey). Under the tunic men wore trousers which were bound to the leg from below the knee, like puttees. Shoes could be quite elaborate, with decorative piercings etc. but for everyday use the labourers probably slipped on a pair of soft leather boots that sagged a bit round the ankles, as excavated at Leatherhead.

Unearthed costume material reveals skill and craftsmanship; everything was made to last and be serviceable. By implication, it had to display the skills of the manufacturer but whether clothing was made exclusively by the women or whether men were adept at tailoring is unknown. Colour wise, cloth was dyed blue or green with additional colours (from scarce and expensive dyes) reserved for strips of intricate designs of tablet weave that were sewn onto garments as edging. Dress for special occasions or for specialist occupations is unclear. Even the vestments of the priesthood are unknown but when Rogers draws attention to the

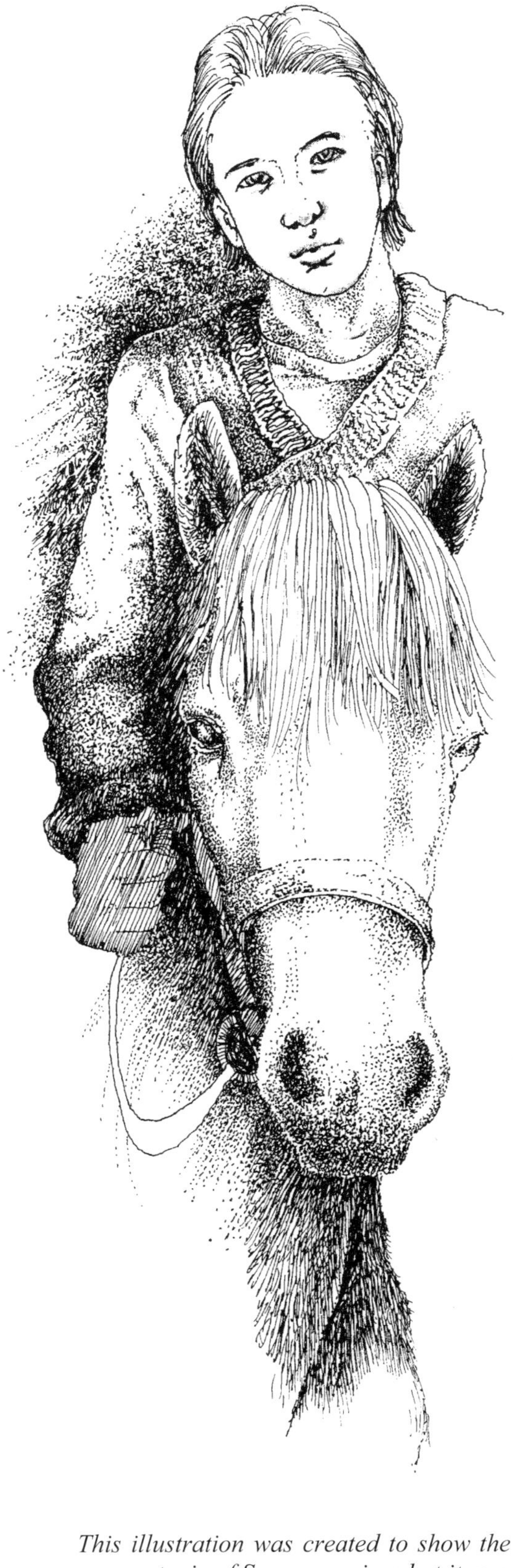

This illustration was created to show the cross-over tunic of Saxon warriors but it may well be premature since it is believed this did not become fashionable until the 7th century.

Illus. opp. of the bowman is also arguable since it does not seem to be known for sure how long the bow was at this period.

finds of male skeletons with 'dress' brooches and describes these as 'cross-dressing' is she not possibly identifying priests, with their vestments pinned at the shoulders in the same way as of a woman? In later times priests become distinctive in the landscape because they were not allowed to carry weapons whereas other men carried shields and spears. Several writers have said that these were carried 'at all times' which is a ridiculous statement. Workmen needed freedom to use their hands. Perhaps the knife at the belt sufficed. Are we to imagine the ploughman had his spear and shield lying beside the field? If that were so then the theory of peaceful acculturation falls apart. Farmers could carry their

bow and arrows more conveniently and probably did, for vermin control or procuring wild meat, as and when opportunities arose. It looks as though bows were low status since among grave goods they are far outnumbered by shields and spears. It does not look as though there was a rite of passage from being a bowman to a spearman because graves have been found of small boys with short spears, leading some archaeologists to wonder whether the provision of spears and shields in the grave indicates membership of a distinct social class.

All menfolk knew their place in society and the responsibilities that went with it. They walked out proudly and walked tall too. Saxon men were not small. They stood some 5ft 10in to 6ft, calculated from excavated skeletons (although there were many shorter men too). Having been labouring since childhood, they had broad shoulders and muscular limbs to go with the height. It would not have been a good idea to upset one! A prime source of their pride lay in their ability to provide not only protection for their family group but their food. Nearly all of them were farmers but the most multi-skilled farmers imaginable. These were men who knew how to work the land in its entirety and as a renewable resource too. They could manage all the livestock and all the crops covered in this book plus the working and maintenance of coppice woodland and hedgerows, with a wisdom that is rapidly becoming a national rarity in today's England of specialisations. Even the Saxon specialists would have been general practitioners too. The great distinction was in their over-view of the whole landscape. It was a god-given land and of that there were constant reminders when every day was dedicated to particular pagan deities who would influence every minute of it. Today, in a world that has now become increasingly secularised, many have no belief in the constant presence, influence and interference of supernatural forces but to the pagan Saxons it was all a sacred landscape – and they were part of it.

WOMENFOLK

Meet Ælfred's wife. Just as Ælfred had been to gather holly for the midwinter celebrations, so his wife had been to collect elder blossom for the crowning of the summer king at the summer solstice.[2] Her position as 'wife' is uncertain, for when St. Augustine wrote from Canterbury in 604 to ask Pope Gregory the Great what he should do about the Saxons continuing to hang up evergreens at Christmas, the Pope replied that they could be Christianised and what Augustine needed to concentrate upon was abolishing the multiple marriages.

If she was the 'chief' wife of the house then she ruled it. For this her Saxon society awarded respect and honour. It was she who, according to their custom, welcomed all visitors whether stranger or known. It was she who served up hospitality and passed among the guests with the ale or mead. Woe betide anybody who drank too much and caused offence, for this woman had muscles to back up her authority. Like all the other farm wives, she toiled on the land alongside her man, developing such powerful muscles that their bone attachments enlarged, to the marvel of later archaeologists. Farm labouring duties were on top of her farmhouse duties of running the home and raising children, and most important of all was the baking of decent bread. That was reflected in her word for 'lady' which was *hlæfdige,* derived from 'bread-kneader'. Men took responsibility for working the land while their women were responsible for the meals. Those centred on bread. Any meat, butter, cheese, eggs, fruit or vegetables were viewed as accompaniments.

Of course running a home does not leave much of an imprint in the archaeological record and so we have to wait until documentation becomes available and hope we can identify traditional values. Precious little of the early writing reflects home life but we get a little from their poetry. Although poetry was idealised it would reflect tradition to ensure the audience recognised and related to the content. Even so, there are some tantalising questions that remain unanswered. For example, we do not know whether her household duties put her in charge of textiles: the carding, spinning, weaving and clothes-making. In later medieval times the women span and the men wove but then it was an industry whereas out on early Saxon farms much of the output would have been for home use. No records indicate whether production was divided by gender but with so much for a farmer's wife and mother to do it would be reasonable to guess that on dark winter evenings the men wove. Two surnames have devolved from this, Weaver and Webster, often

treated as though they devolve from the same occupation, whereas websters are likely to have set up the web of warps and wefts into which the weavers wove. Those tasks could have been separated by gender. We'll never know. What does look likely, from archaeological evidence, is that where farmsteads made up a village then one of the buildings was a weaving house where the women gathered to work together. Doubtless any news was carded thoroughly too and when they ran out of gossip they probably sang. Young girls learned the words needed for playing their part after communal meals in the leader's hall, when the story-teller (*scop*) came to the fore, accompanied on the harp. It looks as though *scop* and harpist were largely male provinces, so women probably provided the choral accompaniments. They are hardly likely to have been excluded from all music.

In regions beyond Surrey (East Anglia, the Midlands and the North East) archaeologists find that some women, but not all, wore something special from their belt. These get recorded as 'girdle hangers' and usually occur in pairs but we have no idea as to their function. Nobody has come up with a practical use so they were probably symbolic, perhaps symbolising married status but doubted seeing as some wearers were only about fifteen. It is not known for certain when girls married but it is believed they were at least eighteen An alternative suggestion would have the girdle-hangers symbolising that she was the eldest woman of the household and therefore in charge However, in either of these situations they ought to be commonplace in graves and they are not. Intriguingly, each pair found has been different, as though they were very personal and therefore a connection with romance and marriage may well be right. As none have been found for the Saxons of Surrey we are left wondering how these people conveyed the same message; something must be missing from my drawings of women. They did not wear wedding rings. One obvious possibility is that hair-styles were used, with girls having long hair left showing, until covered with a veil/headdress upon marriage. If the headdresses were worn before marriage then maybe they were colour coded. Certainly there must have been some sort of signal; Saxon England was not the place for illegal liaisons.

Upon marriage, the women took on the identity of their man and became a member of his extended family and tribe, in return for their protection. It was they who had negotiated the terms of her marriage settlement on her behalf, before the suitor then paid up his *morgengifu* (morning gift) to her (not to her father). She was free to do as she pleased with it, whether keep it, sell it or gift it. Thus within the marriage both parties could hold wealth independently of each other, but should divorce arise then she had the rights to half their joint holding, and she could take her children with her.[3]

It used to be thought that there must have been many mixed marriages between Saxons and Romano-British following the mass migrations; that Saxon warriors left the women back home and so had to take a British wife. That is now doubted on several grounds but with modern science (working with teeth) making it possible to determine where somebody had spent their childhood we should learn much more about the folk movements. Of course that theory did help explain the rapid establishment of a Saxon society since a British wife took on the identity of her Saxon husband and doubtless was expected to raise their children as Saxons. Crucially that would mean all of them learning the Saxon language. Doubtless speaking Romano-British in a Saxon home would not have been acceptable and that must have been such a trial to British wives there, bringing up their first baby and not knowing 'baby talk' in anything but her own language. We can almost hear the father snapping "I do not want to hear that word in my house again." Similarly, speaking British in public must surely have been taboo (as when the English were suppressing Welsh) and so that first generation of wives must have had a few problems in the market place.

Right - It is not known whether the women removed their headdresses in the privacy of their own homes, nor is it known how they sewed since no thimbles have been found but there are more tweezers than expected, leading to the suggestion that they were used for sewing and this proved successful when tested.

CHILDREN

Childhood was a brief affair. There's always more to do on a farm than daylight allows and so as soon as possible after giving birth a mother would return to her work. Babies were probably slung up her back, as in the later Middle Ages, while toddlers stumbled along behind her as best they could. Thus children were initiated into adult working life right from the start and doubtless liked to help with whatever mum or dad were doing. Soon they would be left to do it themselves. Thus they all learned 'general practice', whether by observation or participation, irrespective of gender. That put them in good stead for the rest of their lives, whether they ultimately became a specialist or not. Everybody knew everybody else's job and so there was no escaping criticism. Farms were full of dangers, ranging from germs to open fires, and judging by evidence from graves, it was especially dangerous for toddlers. Overall, about a third of the children died before reaching adulthood.

At what age youngsters were considered to have reached adulthood we do not know, nor what form any rites of passage took. That said, in some instances archaeologists have noticed that graves take on the appearance of an adult's grave when the deceased was 12-14 years old. It is thought that they became of marriageable age in their late teens and certainly many girls did not live much beyond this - the burial grounds have far more skeletons of young women in their early twenties than young men, bringing to mind the dangers of childbirth. Despite these high mortality rates the Early Saxon population expanded so the young women must have been constantly pregnant.

Life on the farm was busy for everybody and that included children, who could never have been bored with all the skills of everyday life to learn. At least some of those were enjoyable, like preparing the clay from which their elders would make pots. Children love playing with clay and doubtless we are right to imagine them sitting round a pile kneading out the stones and roots, pounding in tempering agents, and calling out that it was ready when it wasn't. Eventually they would be allowed to tear off a large lump and roll it into a ball before thrusting their thumbs into the top and start squeezing out the sides into a small thumb-pot. Making sausages of clay was fun too, ready for adults to coil them round and round to create a larger pot, pressing coil into coil as they went. Next came the decoration, from the pressing of carved wood or bone tools into the clay to create patterns of indentations and incised lines; children biting their bottom lips with concentration if they were allowed to have a go. With great care these were placed somewhere safe to dry out for a few days; under cover if rain threatened. As the outer surfaces dried they could be burnished, to give them a more shiny 'finished' appearance, but which also compressed the clay somewhat to increase success in the firing. For firing there was the trench left from last time and so the next task was to fetch fuel. Pots and fuel were layered into the trench and dad cut turves with which to cap the lot when ignited. The clamp smouldered slowly for a couple of days, baking the pots unevenly, so that they would come out blackened on the hot side, red on the cooler side, but always a delight to the children. The big funerary urns used after cremation rituals may have been the work of a specialist and maybe the designs impressed were a sort of 'heraldry' that could be read.

Looking at these pots today, they appear quite ugly, when other everyday things were fashioned so beautifully. Another surprise is the Saxons not throwing pottery on a wheel (yet) even though they understood, made and used wheels for their vehicles, even though they practised shaping in circular motion when it came to wood-turning on a pole-lathe. Even the simplest of bowls turned on a pole-lathe is a thing of beauty and perhaps that is why the pots appear to be of such poor quality. Perhaps they were seen as short-lived, utilitarian wares whereas things for longer life were of turned wood. There was a long tradition of wood turning, with the British in Surrey eating from plates and bowls way before the Romano-British period and indeed before some other British tribes. Saxon ideas would have been an extension of this.

Children could have stood by the pole lathe and watched a length of wood being turned in a replicated design ready for cutting into a series of identical pieces – the little men for their board games. It was not all work. Early Saxons played too and enjoyed board games, judging from the gaming pieces found. The notion that games requiring dice were probably rare, since so few have been recovered, ignores the likelihood that most would have been made of wood and rotted away or were destroyed in the funeral pyres and not come through to us in cremation deposits. Saxons could have played Nine Men's Morris too, for that is far older, but anyone wanting to experience the emotions of an early Saxon should try their game of *hnefatafl* (king's table) which was popular all over North West Europe (and is available commercially today; sold sometimes as 'Viking chess'). It is played with unequal

sides where the larger side has to capture the king of the smaller side but the king is permitted moves denied the others. It's either a simple game for children or an infuriation for adults intent on tactics!

Other toys are even rarer and must have been made of organic materials but it does not sound as though the children had much time to themselves so perhaps toys amounted to little more than a rag doll with which to go to sleep. They had pets since the farm dogs would have littered a succession of puppies but to what extent these, or indeed any of the other farm animals, were raised as pets is debatable. Cat bones have been excavated and cats were doubtless valuable for vermin control. Saxons shared their homes with the house mouse and the wood mouse but there were no brown rats yet and even the black rat had only arrived recently, with the Romans' ships. Their bones have been found in places like London, Southampton and York, suggesting these mammals were still restricted to the ports.

How children were dressed is a great uncertainty since an outfit of children's clothing has yet to be discovered. It is thought they were dressed as little adults. In graves we find a few beads from a necklace but only a *few* beads. Occasionally a brooch turns up and these are usually, but not always, adult size. Boys were buried with a spear sometimes, like their fathers, and these are occasionally child-size. A fighting man was a *cempa* giving rise to 'kemps' or 'kempers' as English regional names for the children's combat game played with the flowering stalks of ribwort plantain. Each player took turns to try and strike off the head of his opponent's plantain with his own (*illus. p.24).* Thus in some northern dialects 'to kemp' means to fight and there are parallels in other languages of N. W. Europe too. Blowing dandelion 'clocks', if played, would certainly have been to different words as the farm day was not divided into hours. The game has been updated. So have the nursery rhymes, such as 'Rock-a-bye Baby', which is of unknown origin but far older than so frequently stated. Linguists say it has a Saxon rhyming scheme and rhythm. That would tie in with its links to the midwinter rituals, since the tree is supposed to be the holly. Thus right from the outset children were inducted into their culture and childhood was seen as an apprenticeship towards their being full members of society.

They would experience their society outside their own communities at the great seasonal gatherings, which would have amounted to far more than simply religious rituals. Activities are likely to have been gender based. It is easy to imagine girls working alongside mum at trading textiles but it is likely that all aspects of dairying and poultry were their province too, leaving the men to strike bargains over oxen and horses. With horses becoming increasingly important through the troubled times of establishing the Saxon kingdoms it was imperative that the fitness of the horses was shown off and seeing as horse racing had been invented it is not difficult to imagine boys showing off their prowess at the same time, as lightweight jockeys. It still happens in the few surviving horse fairs across Europe. Then the boys could pitch themselves against each other in wrestling matches. It was important that those new recruits showed off not only that they were fit for society but that they were desirable.

SLAVES

That so much of the famous English countryside was created by slave labour is not a fact that comes to mind very readily today. To have watched people working the fields in Saxon times would have meant overseeing the slaves. It was not a new idea. The Romans had slaves and to any Saxon immigrants it would not have been novel either for they had slaves in their homelands too. When the system began is not clear but one suggested possibility has the Saxons adopting the idea from over their southern border from the Romans. Whatever the origins, it absolved some people from doing a lot of hard work and could provide extra revenue too, since surplus people could be sold in the markets; they were owned as chattels and traded as such. It provided a useful solution to prisoners of war too, for although warriors could be ransomed or executed there was still the problem of disposing of women and children. They were given a choice: death or slavery.

Saxons built a class society of eight levels, with prescribed degrees of freedom for each except the lowest level – the *theow* or slaves. However, as society evolved in England so they were given rights and their lot was not necessarily as bad as we might imagine, given that our concept of slavery has been coloured by that of the American plantations. Their

owner had to feed, house and protect them, in return for their labour, but it was not in his best interests to treat them so harshly as to breed insurrection. Doubtless there were decent owners and brutal owners

Tracing these people is almost impossible but observations in archaeology reports that women's skeletons were deformed by hard labour does suggest these were slave women, or had been in their younger days. There were options for escaping slavehood. Laws were passed to allow slaves to buy their way out (fat chance) or they could be granted their freedom by bequest through the dying wishes of their owner, in recognition of their loyalty, or they could redeem themselves through hard work. The last instance arose in several ways. The courts sometimes condemned the guilty to a period of slavery as their punishment, or, debtors were allowed to work off the debt.

When slaves had children they too were born into slavery (upon marriage a woman took on the class of her new husband). That ensured stability in the social system and kept the supply going cheaply, for slaves were not cheap in the markets. There was a ready demand for them from abroad that kept the prices high. Also to maintain social stability was the option of persons placing themselves into slavery for reasons of security. That normally applied to a woman who was not welcomed back into her extended family when her husband died and left her without protection. She could then turn to any other man for a home and security in return for labour. There was no other social provision for the destitute (although the option of becoming a nun in an early Christian monastery cannot be ruled out). In famine years parents could save some of their children from starvation by putting them into slavery.

In the days when the mass migration theory was unchallenged then it was presumed that the Romano-British were enslaved by the conquerors to continue working the land. That has to be reassessed now and has implications for understanding place-names. The Saxon word for 'foreigner' (*wealh*) was used of the British, giving us 'Welsh' and the 'wall' on the end of Cornwall, but it occurs also as a prefix to place-names associated with the British, such as Walton-upon-Thames and Walton-on-the-Hill in Surrey. In due course it came to mean 'slave'.

Any idea of rebellion was curbed by the death threat and even after the conversion to Christianity there were no penalties for killing slaves. Any rebellious ideas of overwhelming and killing the whole overlord family were curbed by the way Saxon society worked. The intense family loyalty reached beyond the immediate household to include all the extended family and all of those collectively as the tribe. Each person had to take responsibility for all the others and so if one crossed the law and incurred a penalty all the family chipped in to pay. This intense bonding led to blood feuds between families to avenge murders and ultimately warfare between tribes. To the slaves it meant that if you upset one Saxon you upset the lot. There was no escape.

How to distinguish a slave from a freeman seems to be unrecorded but surely, in such a strict class society, there was a way. It would have legal implications in the market place when transacting deals. If it is intangible to the archaeologists then possibly it was the colour of their garb, with slave costumes not being dyed (cheapest option). We will probably never know. What is certain is that slavery persisted right through the whole Saxon era until eventually the Christian Church persuaded William the Conqueror to abolish it at the Council of Westminster in 1102.

END NOTES

1 Gelling and Cole list the following:- Anningsley from Anna, Billeshurst from Bill, Bletchingley from Blæcca, Englefield from Inga, Gomshall from Guma, Paddington from Pada, Pitch Font from Pic, Tatsfield from Tatel, Tilford from Tila (uncertain), Tillingdown from Tilla (deduced), Titsey from Tydic (deduced), Willinghurst and Wonersh from Willa. Although unattested, Dunsfold comes probably from a personal name such as Dunt. Gelling and Cole were working nationally; dip into a volume specific to Surrey (Gover *et al*) and more surface.

2 The pagan midsummer celebrations were so important that the Christians had to adopt them and converted the festival to the Feast of St. John the Baptist, since he heralded the birth of Christ six months beforehand just as the pagans crowned their Midsummer king six months before the midwinter king. The elder became one of the sacred plants of St. John, known as 'the herbs of St. John'. See Howkins 1996.

3 Æthelbert's Law 79. As king of Kent this custom was likely to have prevailed in Surrey too, certainly when Surrey was ruled by Kent. His Law 77 protects against deception over the marriage settlement, saying, '*if there be guile, let him bring her home again, and let his property be restored to him.*'

GOATS AND GODS

Goats are fun. They have smiley mouths. They look at you quizzically out of yellow eyes with weird rectangular pupils. There are not so many to be seen in Surrey nowadays and certainly not the wandering goat-herd with twenty or more, which would have been a familiar scene in Saxon times. These were animals valued for their milk, butter, cheese, meat, sinew, fat and grease, hides and hair, bone and horn, and dung for the land or for fuel – very useful animals. When it came to meat, the bones unearthed by archaeologists are most often of young goats, suggesting the female kids went into the dairy herds while most male kids were culled and eaten. The butchered bones of mature goats are rare; nobody wanted to eat an old goat.[1]

Crucially they are browsers rather than grazers so they do not need quality pasture but prefer a goodly mixture of rank weeds and twiggy stuff. That made them ideal beasts for pioneer settlers who could not afford cattle or good pastures. Goats could subsist on the rough ground surrounding the fields and woods and thereby make it productive. Quite probably they were farmed extensively on the heathlands, especially in the winter, since goats are enthusiastic about nibbling off young Scots Pines and the pines disappear from the record by mid Saxon times. Where farmland was expanding into woodland goats could have been employed to clear the undergrowth ready for tree removal in the winter. In appearance the goats looked like today's except for being a bit shorter. Their coats were long and often black and since they are the only domestic animal that reverts to the wild if they escape so the several herds of feral goats in Britain give us a glimpse of Saxon times.

The name comes straight from the Saxon *gat* and occurs in Surrey place-names[2] such as Gatton and several Gatwicks. However, Carole Hough[3] has proposed that there was another *gat* word, now lost, which can be deduced from plant names, since the dogwood[4] was known as gatter-bush in Kent, gatter-tree in Lincolnshire, gatteridge in East Anglia and Southern England. This dispersal of names covers centres of Jutish, Anglian and Saxon cultures suggesting the origin of the name was something commonplace, both within and among the cultures and that could well have been goats. In Kent, Eastern and Southern England, gatteridge and gatter-tree have been recorded for the spindle-tree also but this could have arisen from the two shrubs being cropped for the same purposes. Primarily, they were coppiced to provide good withes for weaving cradles and baskets.

So Gatton could have meant the place where they herded goats on the Downs or where thickets of dogwood were managed as a resource? The link is more likely with goats. They were so commonplace that to get a place-name must surely imply there was something special going on there and the answer to that may lie with pagan religious practices. Those need to be explored if we are to have any chance of seeing the landscape as the Saxons saw it. To them it was a sacred landscape. That is difficult to grasp today when our culture is saturated with scientific explanation rather than governance by supernatural forces. Goats provide a starting point for seeing Surrey through Saxon eyes.

From Gatton Park (*illus. above*) the view south is impeded by the ridge of Redstone Hill and out beyond that lies the clay Weald and the airport at Gatwick. The element *wic* seems to have been used for trading centres, such as ports (*Hamwic;* Southampton, and *Lundenwic* London), while others were markets and some were specialist farms. The Gatwick farms specialised in goats, which were not low status animals in Early Saxon times. They even had sacred roles, with a pair drawing the chariot of such eminent gods as Woden and Thunor, who were mighty sky gods of ancient origin, manifesting themselves in thunder and lightning and the pattern of the stars in the night sky.

The great sky gods were revered at a sacred site beside Gatwick, at Horley, evidenced by the name Thunderfield (Thunor's field) and a medieval document of 1273 refers to a nearby hill by its Saxon name of *Wedreshulle* or Woden's Hill.[5] These were remote places but that was crucial to many pagan rituals, especially those centred upon trees and woodland.[6] The Horley area was indeed part wooded as per the name of the next village, Charlwood. The first element of that name comes straight from the Saxon *ceorl* (pronounced charl) which was the land-owning rank in the class-structured society. Part of the Wealden forest had been felled hereabouts to give the clearing or 'ley' of Horley and so places like Thunderfield Common are believed by Gavin Smith to have been open common pasture lands, in which case Woden's Hill should have been clearly visible. Somewhere thereabouts may have been a social group serving the temple and intriguingly, the nearby settlement of Burstow has a name that meant a fortified place or the meeting place at the stronghold. This suggests that at some point during the cultural changes there was an expectation of conflict but there is no early document surviving to give dated guidance as to when Burstow came into being. Possibly any strife arose, not so much from new peoples as from new religious ideas. Overall, the archaeology suggests continuity and indeed it seems to have become a site of lasting importance if Thunderfield has been identified correctly as the *thunresfelde* of the Royal Council meeting in the 930s.[7] Soon after that it must have gone into decline, for the Normans recorded no indications of any of this in the Domesday Book of 1086. Significantly, for the current reassessments of the 5th and 6th centuries, this site combines that of religious centre and royal vill and that recurs in other significant places in Surrey, including Godalming which shall be reviewed shortly.

Before that though, we seem to have lost sight of the goats but they have been there all the time, at Gatwick.

In religious rituals goats have featured for thousands of years, as sacrificial animals, persisting in today's notion of a 'scapegoat'. Thus we can deduce that there was this extra dimension to the demand for goat kids, with the likelihood that the Gatwick farm specialised in their production for the local temple.

Although purely speculative it is possible that the goat herds from Gatwick were moved seasonally up on to the Downs to Gatton; perhaps in the winter to get the animals out of the hideous wet Wealden clay. There are certainly place-name clues to the seasonal movements of livestock in earlier times, known as transhumance, including 'winter' names such as Winterfold, up on the drier sandstone hills.[8] We know also that places like Merstham next to Gatton and Sutton to the north, had their *denns* or pig-pasturing places, to the south, at Thunderfield.[9] Therefore, as we try to imagine our chosen landscape in those distant times our imaginings need to include the seasonal movements of livestock, and of course the people with them. Perhaps it was an adventurous day out for everybody capable of the miles. The more hands the better. Certainly the boys would have been taken in order to teach them the route, ready for when they too would be the leaders.

Now it's time to get back to the other goat names and turn attention this time from the South East to the South West. Scattered across it are clues and evidence of the ancient pagan religions, with a concentration at Godalming, which became a royal vill too and thus gets identified as one of the 'central places' in the early Saxon period. Part of Godalming is Tuesley and that has a Gatwick Farm, fitting the place into the sacred pattern highlighted earlier. Two other places near Godalming, Eashing and Peper Harow, have religious associations too, as does Elstead to the west, complete with a Gatwick.

To make sense of all these we need to see the landscape through ancient eyes, for it is very distinctive. This becomes apparent when approaching it along the River Wey from the north as

the early Saxons would have done, travelling deep into the southern lands from the Thames Valley and London. Once through the chalk downs at Guildford the look of the land changes and the valley has a surprisingly wide flood plain which was most likely cleared of trees to create pasturage. Ahead the hills close in, with a gap between them through which we guess the river flows. That is the view illustrated above (the river is just off-page on the left) looking up across acres of grassland that is the Godalming Lammas Lands, which were there in Saxon times. To continue following the river upstream we trudge up the left edge of the illustration above and then swing to the right in front of the sunlit tree silhouettes, to pass through the notch of the hills on the far right side. The left hand scarp, rendered dark and without today's rooftops, has Tuesley on it. The right hand scarp is known now as Frith Hill.[10] We can see the view up the valley is 'blocked' by the ridge of a long low hill set further back and this is Ockford Ridge with Upper Eashing on the right hand end overlooking the river.

The little River Ock has cut Ockford Ridge off from the main hill bearing Tuesley and thereby created a set of three hilltops, which must be unique in Surrey. Ancient peoples certainly seem to have considered it significant. They gave great attention to boundaries and here it looks as though we are approaching a boundary, where the Wey has cut a gateway through the hills but it is not open to us. It is blocked by Ockford Ridge. This is highly likely to have been viewed as a special place, not forgetting that the number three has always been sacred. Archaeologists have long viewed Upper Eashing and Tuesley as probable sacred sites and possibly there was another on Frith Hill about which we know nothing. Approaching up the Wey valley, these three hills across the skyline seem to be guardians of the land beyond, especially as the river does not cut straight through but loops round Eashing, making a staggered entrance through to Peper Harow beyond.

Eashing has caught the attention of place-name specialists for decades, with them dismissing the 'Eash' element as deriving from *æsc* for ash trees and then launching into the debate over the 'ing' element. Wait, the ash trees are significant. They were sacred. According to the creation myth current among the pagans of North West Europe, ash trees were the ancestor tree of all men, being tall and straight

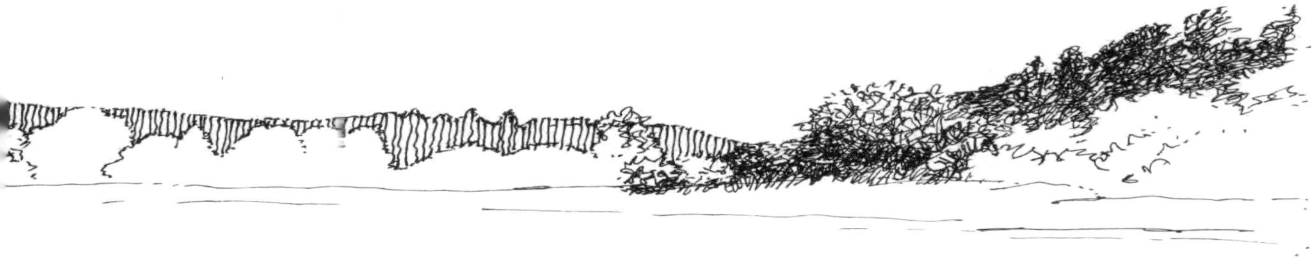

and full of tensile strength (women are descended from the elm tree since both grow bumps on their trunks!). All people on earth were believed to have descended from this primeval pair. Thus at Eashing we have not only the likelihood of a sacred site but we can conclude that it was dedicated to the theme of ancestor worship.

Moving east, across to Tuesley, we have to ford the little River Ock, giving this side of the hill the name Ockford – the Oak tree ford. The Oak tree was sacred to the great sky gods[11] and one of those was Tîw who gave his name to Tuesley, meaning 'the clearing in the oak woods dedicated to Tîw'. He was so important that his sacred day each week is still known as Tuesday. He was a god who wielded the sword and was no doubt popular with Saxon colonists penetrating these parts but at the same time he also wielded his sword to exact capital punishment, telling us immediately that these people were not 'barbarians' as depicted by Roman writers, such as Tacitus, but people who had law and order and justice, even if it differed from our own today.

Moving westwards through the Wey gap, the valley opens out into the water meadows of Peper Harow.[12] The 'harow' comes from *hearg* meaning pagan temple and is quite a rare example. The 'peper' element gave rise to the word 'piper' and has been viewed like a surname of some important pagan associate, perhaps the tribal leader or the high priest. More recently, people like Gavin Smith have suggested we might take it literally and imagine that pipers played an important musical component to the rituals. Now doesn't that stir the imagination! Certainly music had always been important in religious rituals and beautiful Saxon pipes have been unearthed elsewhere. Those that have survived have been of bone, from the limbs of cattle, because they are hollow and come with a natural smooth bore that can give a good note. That means they are relatively short, but wooden ones could have been longer and these would have been made most probably from the strong young growths of the elder tree, since they too are hollow and give a natural bore, much exploited for early musical instruments. Of those excavated, the finger vents numbered three to six, with three being the commonest, suggesting they were played one-handed, leaving the other hand free for another instrument, such as a drum for the rhythm. Of course any pipers at Peper Harow might have played a totally different instrument, akin to bagpipes, for such were in existence by this time. They had also drums and horns so loud music was possible and maybe even necessary because the sacrificial goat kids would have bleated woefully. Even today it makes them unpopular at abattoirs because they sense death and bleat a spine-chilling cry that sounds like a human baby.

Nothing is known about the format of the temple rituals, making them impossible to illustrate. Doubtless much variation existed between different cults and between different temples, involving both men and women priests. It is not even known what the vestments looked like. The detective and reconstructive work of Penelope Walton Rogers makes no mention of the priesthood, although she does have a short section on

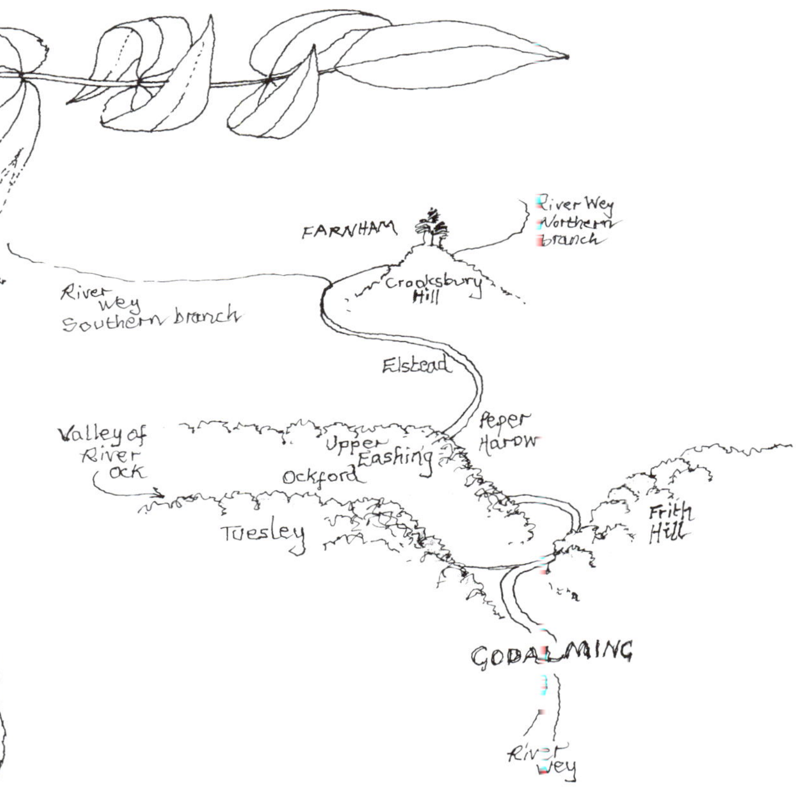

cross-dressing,[13] where graves contain male skeletons in what appear to have been women's clothing, judging by the surviving metal fastenings. Is it not possible that these were priests buried in their vestments? She cites no example of a woman in men's clothing that might indicate that cross-dressing was socially acceptable.

As for the site of the temple at Peper Harow, people have sought archaeological evidence in what is now the Park and not found anything. Possibly the present medieval church was built right over the top of it, as happened elsewhere, but no associated artefacts have come to light from grave digging. It is not likely that the name refers to the temple of ash trees up on top of Eashing hill, overlooking the Park, because that was in a different territory.[14] The chances of finding anything there were reduced greatly in late Saxon times when the site was converted into a defensive burgh; not that there would be much to find if the site was purely a sacred grove. Presumably its priesthood was based in Godalming. They are highly unlikely to have come from over the border. Sadly, evidence of Early Saxon settlements is very difficult to find.

Another intriguing question about Peper Harow is who gave it that name. Place-names are for outsiders since to the insiders it was 'home'. The outsiders in this case must surely have been Christians, using a name of distinctiveness that highlighted religious differences, and that would be in keeping with the general picture of the area. For many a long year it has been noted that there are a lot of pagan associations in South West Surrey, which have been interpreted as indicating residual paganism once Christianity moved in. That was fine in the days when it was believed that Christianity left Britain with the Romans and thereby gave the opportunity for it to 'move in' again at a later date. Now there is archaeological evidence that the faith did not leave but lived on, although in Surrey there is scant evidence for this. Instead, Rob Poulton (*pers.comm*) opines that as it is a Saxon name it must date from after the Saxons took control and as that was at a late date here so by then paganism was usual, hence the distinctive name.

That raises the question as to who used these pagan sites. Although there is much sound argument in forwarding a process of acculturation rather than forceful conquest it does stretch the imagination a bit when it comes to the religious sites. Either the local Romano-British had to adopt the names and rites of the Germanic counterparts of their deities or the two strands of paganism remained separate. With religious belief being held so deeply it suggests they were practised separately, with Christianity soon prevailing over both. That means the Godalming sites are likely to have been of Saxon origin since the names Tîw and Æsc are Germanic. When the broader social pattern is viewed there is evidence that the different social groups were proud of their ethnic differences and perpetuated them, which would surely have included matters of faith. While pondering all this there is that tantalising place-name of Burstow, meaning a fortified place or the meeting place at the stronghold. Against whom were the fortifications raised? Was this pagan against pagan or pagan against Christian zealots or was it separate from the temple site and reflects changes in secular administration? Lots to think about.

If the Godalming sites were established afresh with the incursion of Germanic culture, where were the older Romano-British sites? For the Roman period, there was one to the north at Wanborough but for this part of the Wey Valley the prime possibility would be on the distinctive landmark of Crooksbury Hill, four miles

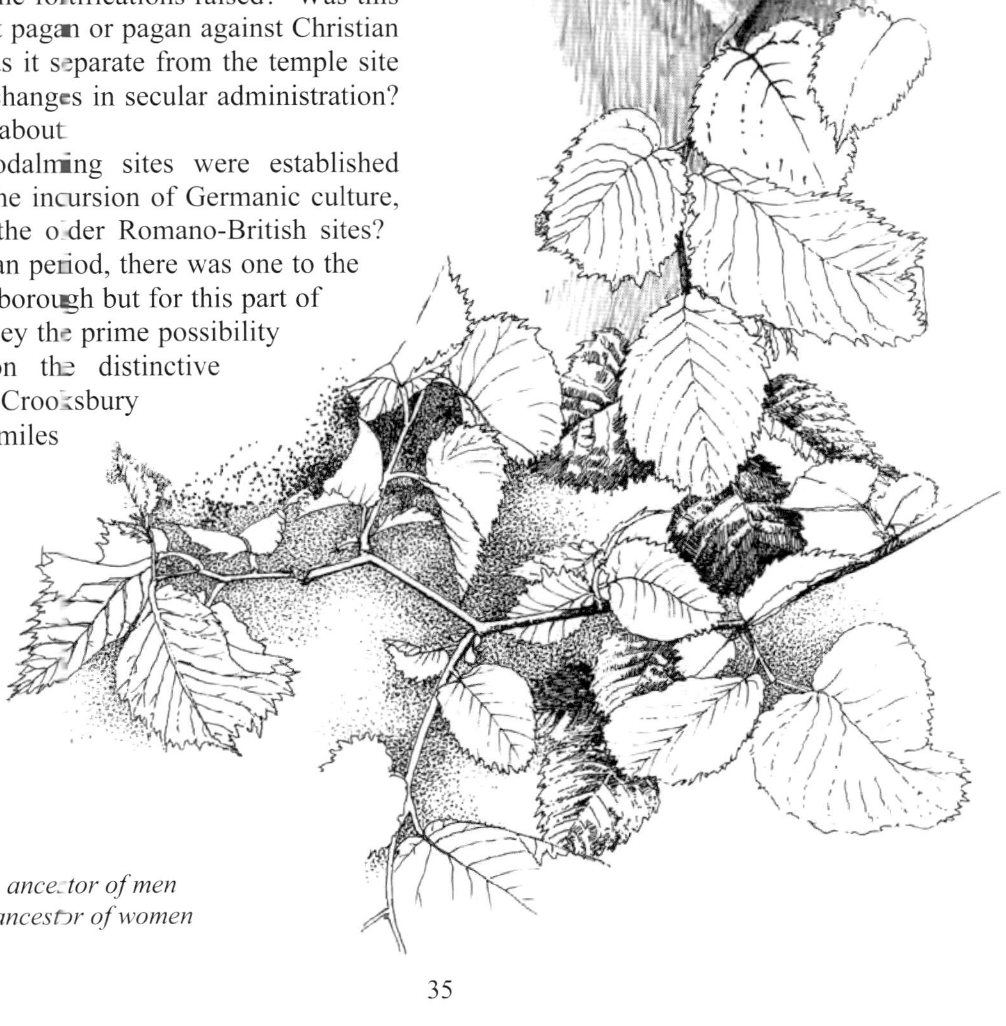

Top-left: Ash, ancestor of men
Above: Elm, ancestor of women

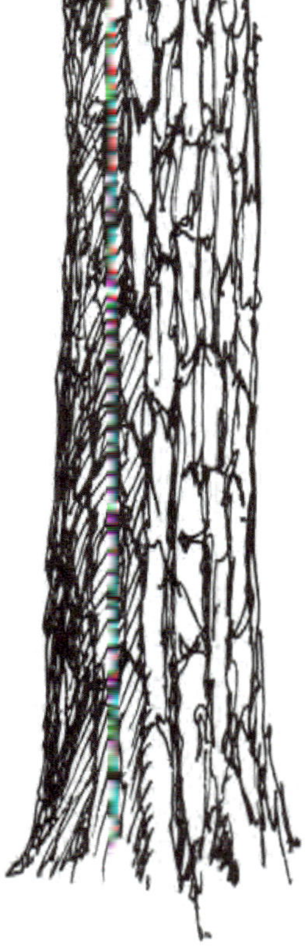

west of the Godalming sites, because the name derives from the British language (*illus. above from below and opposite from summit; from early 20th century photographs*). Round the hilltop are earthworks believed to be ancient (?Late Iron Age) and out on the heath are Bronze Age barrows, so this had been a site of significance for several thousand years.

Hills were important because at least some of the British chose their settlement sites where there was a distinctive one, that they saw as 'the earth's navel' or 'mountain of the world'. Such hills needed to be associated with water as 'waters of destiny'[15] and of course both Crooksbury and Eashing overlook the River Wey. Thirdly, they needed significant trees, to link heaven and earth, such as the sacred ash trees at Eashing and oak trees at Tuesley. There is a third possibility in this area and that is the elder tree, which is thought to have given its name to the village of Elstead in this sacred landscape.

Elstead lies beside the Wey which runs from left to right across the centre of the view sketched (pp.38-9). The landscape is still of trees and heathland, rumpling across to Crooksbury Hill on the skyline, just as in Saxon times. The view was drawn from the heath at Thursley, courtesy of a recent fire that erased the obscuring

foreground birchwoods. Thursley or Thor's ley/ clearing is of course another pagan site. Quite possibly it refers not to the clearing of trees, as is so often presumed, but to the clearing of heather turf to create arable fields. Maybe the Saxons here were indeed immigrants, who turned to Thor/Thunor for protection in the British territory. To a goddess they turned, not only for the comfort of her mothering but as a potent fertility deity for the new arable. Her name was Ellen. Her totem tree was the elder.[16] The settlement dedicated to her – Ellen's homesteads – has been contracted down to Elstead but some place-name experts aver that it refers to the homestead of a Saxon settler, otherwise unknown, with a name like Aella. Sadly there are no surviving documents showing how the Saxons spelt the name, to make it clearer. The earliest is not till 1128. The place-name society volume favoured the

elder tree derivation, without mentioning the other possibility. Sadly we know little about the cult of Ellen in England because the later Christians purged the written record of references to her, doubtless seeing her as a rival to their own Mother Goddess, the Blessed Virgin Mary. On the Continent she was known widely (e.g. as Hyldemoer in Denmark)[17] and there the Christians have been less assiduous in expunging her record. Thus we get glimpses of ideas that would have been brought into the Surrey landscape. Certainly people would have valued the elder, growing by the watercourses, not just for being sacred but for the rich bounty she gave them each year, in terms of wood, foliage, flowers and fruit. This was not only a tasty seasonal food that was highly nutritive but also a rich source of wild yeasts for brewing. The chief brew was mead made from the honey their bees produced after foraging the miles of heather blooms across these heathlands.

We can explore further this relationship between the physical and sacred landscapes hereabouts. A little further west lies the village of Seale. Again there are two favoured derivations for the name. Either it derives from *sele* for hall, indicating an administrative centre, or from *sealh*, meaning the sallow tree (pussy-willow to many people; illus. p.40). Gavin Smith outlines a very convincing argument for the first derivation while Professor Ekwall suggested the second. It's a very interesting suggestion because willows have always been the 'tree of death' and widely so, not just in the Germanic regions but into the Classical mythologies of the Mediterranean too. Could it be that Seale was the place where the local pagans performed their funeral rites? After all, there must have been something special about the willows here since it is in the Wey valley where there must have been miles and miles of willow trees.

The soil at Seale is sand and famously rich in methane gas, giving rise to the weird 'Will-of-the-Wisp' spectacle and to generations of ghostly stories of the supernatural. Surely this would be just the place for the pagans to view as spiritual, as special to the deities and the very place from which to send off their dead to the Other World. In that sense it would be a crucial sacred site in the local territory, and so far nothing has been found elsewhere to suggest a special funerary site. Any archaeological evidence at Seale has been destroyed by the sand extraction that has taken place here for generations – infuriating![18]

The sallow derivation is not incompatible with Gavin Smith's hall theory in terms of local administration by the early Christian Church. Such an important religious site could indeed become an administrative centre, attracting the attention of the Christians who then took it over. Hereabouts they founded the first Minster.[19] There was another minster at Tuesley. Does that tell us that the integration of faiths in the area was peaceful and thus a good place to promote Christianity or was it so pagan that the Church decided it was in dire need of evangelising?[20]

Sallow has always been a harbinger of spring, from the bulging of silver catkins out of the dark brown bud scales to their expansion into gloriously golden powder puffs of pollen, whatever the weather. Although this tree was associated with death, it is difficult to imagine the Saxons finding this a depressing reminder, especially as they had such a sharp eye for natural beauty. Surely golden pussy willow was a reassurance of a better life to come in the Other World, since faiths colour their resurrection beliefs with gold. Green, on the other hand, has been the colour of new life and so the greening of the countryside in the New Year signalled the success of the mid-winter fertility rituals. Greenery was put over a fresh corpse awaiting its funeral and for 'Celtic' peoples the preferred choice was birch. That is what any Saxons immigrants would have found the British doing but almost certainly they brought the same practice with them. The cult of the birch deities was widespread around the northern hemisphere, whether Old World or New World. This was a 'Mother' tree, linking earth with sky and the Other World and known in several guises: the goddess Eostre that became Christianised as Easter, the Celtic Cerridwen/Rhiannon, the Bjork of Iceland and Scandinavia and Freyja to Norse people.[21]

Straight after the Midwinter fertility festival, the sap starts to rise in the birches, full of promise for a new year, and tapping it yielded a reliable safe drink should the frosts have hardened the surface water. What an exhilaration it must have been when the birches on the sombre Surrey heathlands started to flush bright green again. Come autumn they would burnish gold with promise of resurrection. This was not a 'minor' British tree at all.

Elderberry harvest

Its sacred day is unknown. Birch was linked with the moon and could therefore have been honoured on the Moon's Day or Monday. Alternatively, or in addition, the rituals may have been important on Thor/Thunor's Day (Thursday) since in Scandinavia the tree was dedicated to Thor and so presumably with his Saxon counterpart, Thunor. Fertility deities, on the other hand, were honoured on Fridays.

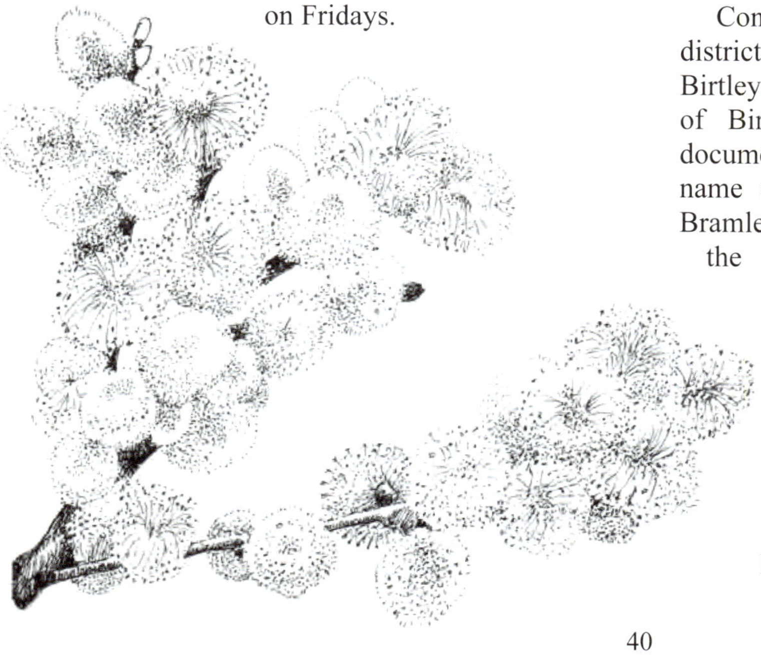

We can guess that the people in the south-western hills of Surrey had great regard for the birch because they have left a collection of associated place-names. These are quite exceptional since birch features rarely in Saxon charters,[22] explained usually in terms of it being relatively short-lived and communal rather than providing distinctive sentinels or boundary markers. It might be that in the Middle Saxon period when Christianity took over and the Church renamed places it wiped out many birch names because of their pagan significance. The manor of Haslemere, however, remained Berchurst (from *beorc hyrst* for birch wood)[23] until the end of the Middle Ages. The manor stands on the lower flank of the hill mass, just above the heavy clays of Holdfast that stretch eastwards to Chiddingfold and the Weald. From this direction early influences seem to have arrived (even in the 13th century the parish of Haslemere was established as a chapelry of Chiddingfold rather than Farnham), so we can imagine pioneers foot-heaving through the clays and seeing birches ahead, signalling drier sands and a good place to stop, with its stream of drinking water just below. The name Holdfast is interesting because it might possibly derive from *holtfæsten*, meaning the stronghold in the wood.[24] The original settlement site that grew into Haslemere has an uncertain location but surely this should join the other proposals in the debate.

Continuing with birch names, there is the district just to the north, of Upper and Lower Birtley. Further north again there are the lands of Birtley House in Bramley, which are documented since 1231 and with the Saxon name are doubtless far older. Intriguingly Bramley itself has fertility connections since the name derives possibly from *brom* meaning the broom shrub, which was another ancient fertility plant?[25] The northern European reverence for the birch would have been a distinction noted by the Romans since the birch was too rare in the Mediterranean to feature in the mythologies of either the Greeks or Romans.

So with the rising sap rose the symbolism of new life and the lengthening of the days,[26] so noticeable by the beginning of February that this became the time of purification rituals to rid the land of evil and ensure another harvest.[27] Other rites were performed, as the season ran up to the important rituals for venerating Eostre, to whom the birch was dedicated. Those rituals were so important they had to be Christianised as Easter. Another set of rituals welcomed in the summer, at the end of April/beginning of May, which the Christian Church would in due course frown down to just one day – May Day. Again the birch played a significant role, as a symbol of light, as a lightning rod between deities and earthlings. Imagine then, the Saxon families setting off to the designated sacred grove of birch trees, carrying seasonal symbolic flowers and branches.[28] Although the birch has been banished as a ritual plant the sallow has not. It was adopted by the Church and so its pussy-willow 'palm' is still cut for church on Palm Sunday – a vestige of those far off days. (*Sallow illus opp. bottom*)

Before leaving these topics, there is another site of possible interest concerning the thunder god, Thunor, and that is Bookham. The god's sacred tree was the oak but on the Continent it was also the beech and this association would have arrived here among the other new ideas. Any migrant Saxons with the beech as a cult tree could well have been disturbed to find that it was so scarce. The Romans had lamented its absence hundreds of years before and the pattern of ensuing agriculture would not have encouraged its spread significantly,[29] to the dismay of Saxons looking for beeches as a sign from Thunor that this was his chosen site for their settlement. One place might have been Bookham, for our words 'book' and 'beech' derive from the same Saxon word. Therefore some archaeologists believe that Bookham was founded in the early pagan Saxon period and that the name reflects the sanctity of the site. However, other archaeologists think Bookham gets its name from being created out of a Late Saxon agreement, with 'book' referring to its written foundation charter. It seems very late to be inserting new estates into the landscape, especially one as big as Bookham, when there was already a string of settlements right along the spring-line from Guildford to Leatherhead. Such a new estate could have been created out of a reorganisation of pre-existing holdings and there is quite a lot of evidence for amalgamation and subdivision of manors in the Late Saxon period, sometimes involving the Church. If that had been the case at Bookham is it not odd that they accepted a name with such pagan associations? To me that suggests that Bookham was established beforehand and was therefore an early settlement.

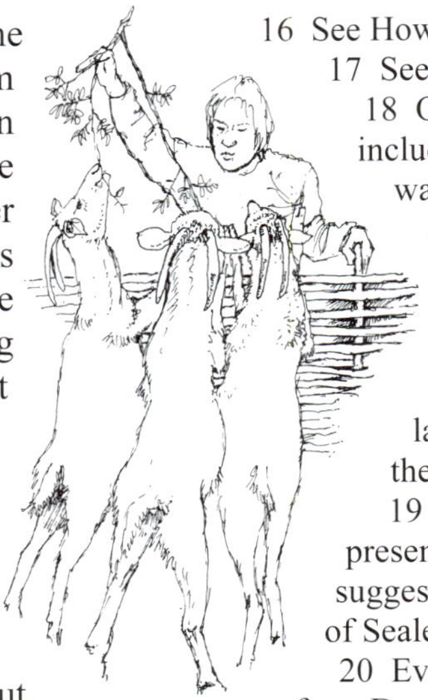

END NOTES

1 Hagen (1995) pp.97-101. Often it is impossible to distinguish bones of goat from sheep.

2 For place-name derivations see Ekwall, Gover, and Smith.

3 Pub. In Biggam.

4 With thanks to Mr C. Podd; see also Grigson.

5 Brit.Lib. Add ch 23516.

6 Blair p.20.

7 See Blair p.19.

8 More information in Smith.

9 Blair p.19.

10 Although frith is a Saxon word it was not applied here until the 19th century, according to Godalming Museum.

11 Howkins 2006. Has more details about the god and the rituals at Tuesley .

12 I am indebted to Rob Poulton (pers.comm) for pointing out that enough is known on early Godalming to know that its boundary did run through here and therefore Upper Eashing was in the Godalming territory whereas Peper Harow was in the territory of the people beyond.

13 Rogers pp. 198-199.

14 pers. com. Rob Poulton.

15 Other Surrey examples in Howkins 1999.

16 See Howkins 1996.

17 See de Cleene, vol I pp. 225-241.

18 Other places named after Sallow include Salfords, south of Reigate, but that was probably a landmark name at a ford although it is very near Gatwick, which might be more significant than we realise. Then there is Cowey Sale at Walton-on-Thames, which is even more likely to be a landmark name since in Saxon times the Thames was tidal up to this point.

19 If the minster was on the site of the present Farnham parish church, as has been suggested, then it was five or six miles west of Seale.

20 Evangelising directed by Bishop Birinus from Dorchester-on-Thames.

21 See de Cleene, vol I, pp 150-162.

22 See Rackham, O. (1986) *The History of the Countryside*; J.M. Dent & Sons Ltd. , London.

23 See Gover p.205.

24 See Gover p.205.

25 Fertility info given in Howkins 2007.

26 This period became 'Lent', from the Saxon *lencten* meaning lengthen, as the daylight hours grew longer. Only the English Saxons were allowed this by the Catholic Church, while the rest of Christendom used names like 'Pasque' derived from 'Pasche' from the Passion of Christ, although that is a borrowing, from the far older Aramaic 'pasha' for the Jewish Feast of the Passover.

27 These did not find favour with the developing Christian Church but to abandon them in favour of Christianity was to take a great risk, especially when there were fresh memories of bad famine years (so severe in 439, 466, 515 and 590 that they were recorded in the Anglo-Saxon Chronicle). The Christians prudently kept the rituals, but Christianised some into Candlemas on 2nd February (Feast Day of the Purification of the Blessed Virgin Mary).

28 In Late Saxon times the Church leant on King Cnut to outlaw these woodland celebrations but the wily English went out before dawn and brought back the plants for home use, hence 'Bringing in the May' rituals, and the Birch was felled and re-erected as the May Pole. Some anthropologists have seen the pole as a phallic symbol which would certainly explain the antipathy from the Church.

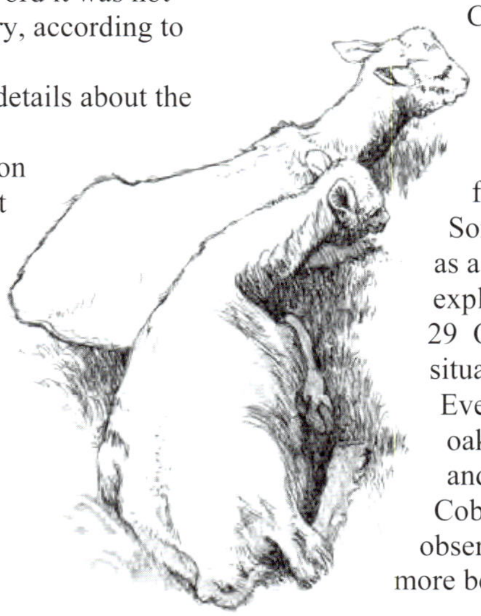

29 Only in the 17th century did the situation start to change. At that time John Evelyn queried why the felling of oakwoods favoured beech rather than oak and in the early 19th century William Cobbett was making the same observations. Since then we have seen more beechwoods than our ancestors ever did.

OXEN, WEALTH AND POWER

It's a simple pleasure to pause and view the beefstock standing motionless in their muddied field with the westerlies ruffling their shaggy winter coats and tumbling the rooks in overhead swirls. To us it is a purely visual pleasure, although the stockman may run a more discerning eye over them as he checks their health. Saxons would have checked for health too but they had an extra dimension to their assessment of such scenes. Just as people today display wealth and social position through consumer goods so the Saxons used cattle. These were their displays of success and wealth and social position.

It was the cattle that had created the very landscape in which they lived, for it was their oxen that worked the pattern of fields in south east England. It was oxpower rather than horsepower that broke the soil for seeding each year's crops just as it had been oxen that had hauled out the tree roots when woodland was converted into fields in the first place. That could have been many generations before Saxon times, since we now understand that the Saxons took over a pre-existing pattern of woods and fields. The old notion of Saxons ripping out the wildwood to create a new farming landscape is erroneous. Indeed there is evidence that agricultural production went into decline during the early Saxon years and it was not until they were well established that there was expansion again. In the early years they simply farmed what they needed in order to sustain themselves. After all, there was no longer a Roman presence demanding taxes and the Early Saxons did not have an extensive export trade so it was less important to produce a large surplus.[1] So often it is described as 'subsistence farming' as though it was only just above survival level and therefore of limited merit. I do not believe for one moment that the Saxons saw it that way. Any who had arrived afresh in the countryside were intent upon making a success of their venture and once they had got land and livestock and were providing for their families they surely thought they were indeed making a success of that venture. For many it must have been a lot better than what they had left behind, so firing their pioneering spirit. Certainly the Anglo-Saxon Chronicles record failure and famine but they also give reasons - crop failure due to inclement weather and crop destruction by storm and pestilence - all beyond the control of the farmers and not reflecting their expertise. The news is still full of such disasters today.

Watching the rooks and cattle in the fields opened up a wonderworld of Saxon life to explore. The following pages look at the types of cattle, the training of oxen as draught animals, the oxherd who looked after them and his assistant dogs, the type of plough and its use, the pasture landscape and the cattle droves across it, together with some of the associated wildlife. However complete or inadequate these explorations might be, they do not take us into the mindset of the Saxons to the extent of appreciating their cattle in their religious terms, for the bull and the cow both had their place in the great pagan allegories.

At least we do not run into a lot of language problems in our explorations of cattle since there was only one term that we cannot define today. Otherwise cattle were so fundamental that we still talk about them in the original Saxon language: bullock, *bulluc*; calf, *cealf*; cow, *cu*; heifer, *heofer*; oxen, *oxan*; and steer, *steor*.

The oxen were not a special breed but simply bull calves that had been castrated, so let us start by asking what the cattle in the fields actually looked like. Firstly, anyone travelling across England would have noticed regional variations in the cattle.[2] Those in the South East are believed to have been black, brought here originally in Neolithic times, and their descendants survive today as the Kerry breed. It is thought that the Romans supplemented those with some different bloodstock and so Saxon migrants who had disembarked at *Lundenwic* would have found visual variety among the animals brought in for slaughter. The Saxons in turn are believed to have shipped over some of their own, which were probably red-coated and survive today as the Sussex breed *(used for opening illus.)*, which can be either black or red. Today's Kerry and Sussex breeds are a few inches bigger than their Saxon ancestors, when an ox was about waist-high to the ploughman. We can still see the Sussex oxen at work at the Weald and Downland Museum in West Sussex.[3] Otherwise, those genes for a red coat have descended to us in such breeds as the Lincolns, Suffolks, Norfolks, Devons, and the Herefords.

Bone by bone, the archaeologists have reassembled the skeletons from the remains in butchers' waste heaps. Thus we know that all were small, at just over 100cm at the shoulder (modern breeds are often half as big again), even allowing for regional variation. Doubtless the larger ones and weaker ones were culled to ensure balance of power in the plough team and temperamental ones would certainly have been taken out. In effect there was selective breeding for uniformity and docility. In appearance the variety was visibly striking in the horns – some didn't have any. There were polled strains already. Others had short-horns, medium horns, or long horns. I've drawn longhorns simply because I like them so much and also because they were there to be drawn at the Weald and Downland Museum. I was surprised the Saxons did not prefer the polled breeds since even a docile animal swinging a head of long horns presented a hazard to the workforce and each other. Maybe the horned ones were kept for virility since I remember being told by one of our foremost breeders of Ayrshire cows that he would never use polled strains because he was certain that they had lost some of their strength and virility.[4] Apart from that, horn was a valuable material, known particularly for drinking vessels and musical instruments but employed also for a multitude of other little tasks, like the teeth for combs. Lots of combs get unearthed by archaeologists so there is nothing new in mums telling their little boys to comb their hair before they go off to start each day of usefulness.

To get a little closer to those times we could try going to Chaldon, up on the chalk hills north of Reigate. The name comes from 'calves' down', meaning the place on the downs where the calves were pastured.[5] Calves must have been pastured on many of the downs, especially in this north-eastern area since it was a region of more intensive farming. What then was so special about Chaldon?[6] Could it have been a place where they specialised in breeding the imported cattle from the continent? Presumably somebody got on with doing that somewhere; after all, they were valuable, high status animals. Obviously they were considered 'better' animals in some way. They would therefore require extra protection from rustlers, and that implies hedged enclosures. Thus Chaldon might not have been simply an important rearing/trading farmstead but also have created a different look to the landscape.

For hedging the Saxons used hawthorn, which derives from their *haga thorn* or 'hedge-thorn'. No doubt it was chosen for its armoury of thorns and alacrity at resprouting if damaged or browsed. These practicalities would have over-ridden any of the religious associations with the protective/fertility deities. These were viewed probably as a bonus rather than a deciding factor. Maybe the Saxons believed that as the tree was born out of a bolt of lightning[7] so it would protect against transgressors in a similar way. The only alternative would have been the other sacred thorn, the blackthorn, but that is less easy to control as a hedge and it would have expanded out into the enclosed grassland by suckering madly. Trying to grow the two together is rarely successful; something that must have been discovered at a very early date as it features in Greek mythology.[8] Therein we find that Eris (blackthorn) caused strife for her twin brother Ares (hawthorn illus. p.46) and so the two should not be left alone together.[9] Today, beyond the suburban fringe of Chaldon, there are still pastures redolent in May with the scent of hawthorn. The logic behind it being regarded as a prime fertility plant lies probably in the way that after pollination the scent of the blooms changes to one that reminds some people of sex. It was so important in the fertility rituals for welcoming in the summer, in May, that the tree had its name changed to 'May blossom' and the name of the month was changed to May from the earlier *thrimilci* - the month when they milked the cows three times a day. The Christians clamped down on this pagan season, grudgingly allowing but one day, May Day, for the 'bringing in of the May' but promoting the notion that to bring in May blossom was unlucky. It's far from unlucky to be up on the Downs near Chaldon on a beautiful May morning, when the hedges are white with bloom and the air is ringing with

the song of the larks. The Saxons enjoyed that too. We don't know their names for all the birds but they certainly wrote about the lark – *lawrice*.[10]

If we now turn an eye to the more general pastures we can travel to Godalming where the riverside Lammas Lands at the end of the town are left as pastures, much as they must have been in Saxon times. In recent years they have been grazed by small black cattle, which although modern Aberdeen Angus crosses, have nevertheless given a 'Saxon' look to the scenes. In 2007 there were mares and foals, illustrated in the hay chapter. Otherwise we could go to Ripley where the long village green, running behind the main street, is left as rough grassland till it runs into encroaching woodland at the northern end. That stretches about two thirds of a mile, and with trees round so much of it evokes those far off times when woods were cleared to make the first great pastures. The eye-stretching length of the green at Dunsfold, complete with wild flowers and drooping grasses and little ponds where the cattle could drink, is evocative too. So are the greens and ponds at Cranleigh, even though not left so rough, needing only a blink of imagination to dot them with little black cattle, ripping the forage against their teeth with their tongues, in that rhythmic noisy way of theirs.

We would know exactly where more of these pastures were if only we knew for sure what the Saxons called them! The suggestion[11] is that place-names ending in *leah,* that give us the –ley/leigh endings, were not just 'clearings' but clearings used as rough pasture, giving rise to the heather grazing on the sandy commons, like Headley and Wisley, and grass pasture on the clay commons like Horley and Cranleigh. The claylands stretching south across the Surrey Weald into Sussex were probably used extensively for cattle ranching and so we should imagine miles of rough pasture between the woodlands across these lowlands. The clays were too heavy for early ploughs, and were rather acidic and infertile for cropping anyway. They cracked wide in hot summer droughts to ventilate the Underworld, while in winter they grabbed victims by the feet. Such clays sneered at cultivation. They sported forest till people cleared swathes for pastures and throve on cattle ranching. Using them for forestry and grazing was the ideal solution and one practised already by the Romano-British. Even today Cranleigh's massive sweep of greens with little ponds is easy to imagine as rough grass with little black or red cattle gathered around one of the watering holes, with the oxherd and his dogs watching over them.

The oxherd would have seen more than the cattle. The rough grazing on wet soil made the favoured haunt of that pokey-nosed bird, the snipe. To the Saxons it was a *snite*, meaning a long, thin object, and one look at the illustration leaves no doubt as to what they had in mind. By day it is not an easy bird to see as it lies up resting but come dusk and out it comes to feed, probing busily with that long

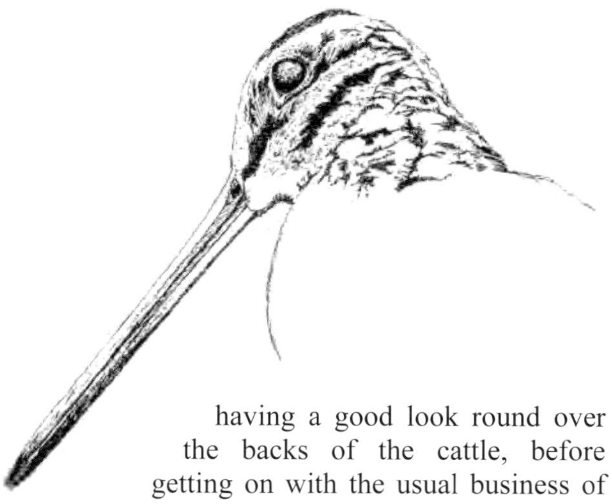

bill for prey such as earthworms. They can be plentiful in a cow pasture. All through the nightly hours they work away before returning to rest ahead of the rising sun. They still favour the rough grazing on the Godalming Lammas Lands. The Saxons took them as food; their bones turn up in butchers' rubbish heaps.[12] Also in the heaps have been found the bones from birds of prey, like the red kite and the peregrine falcon, which may be a clue as to how some of the snipe were caught. Hawking has always been elitist though and so might not have been a frequent sight in Early Saxon Surrey.

There was another bird he saw too. When thick mists made a moon of the early morning sun he would hear the echoey clamourings of the first formations coming in over the diffused shadows of their wide, grey wings. He'd see their long legs swing down and then, with hardly a hesitation, bounce on their stilts as they landed in the grass. The cattle took no notice. They were used to the cranes. The frogs and voles were not. They dived aside a grazing muzzle but with the cranes they leapt into oblivion, bill-stabbed from above. The cranes would raise their heads and swallow, having a good look round over the backs of the cattle, before getting on with the usual business of worm-hunting. The oxherds among their cattle knew them well, got close enough to see the red patches on their heads, got to calling this place 'the crane's clearing or *leigh*' - Cranleigh.[13]

Thus the migrating cranes spanned darknesses of forest, linked by the drove roads for shifting swine from wood to wood. Between the woods the paler grasslands rolled and swathed where grazing herds could wander at feed, as was their natural way. Hungry wolves needed to venture far from tree-cover to get a calf. Across all this, from time to time, the cranes espied families of people trudging to the religious centres. Soon they'd see red-clad Saxon war-bands galloping across, while picking ravens whitened the skulls of heads on stakes.

Let us leave the grazing lands for a while and turn our attention onto the oxen working the fields. With cattle being so important, the crucial lessons of a Saxon boy's education centred on the skills of handling them. It was through these skills that the boy would be able to fulfil the man's role of providing the corn for the women to convert into bread. Bread

was the meal. Anything else, whether meat or fish, eggs or cheese, fruit or vegetables, was simply an extra, for flavouring, variety and health. Thus the boys would have looked forward eagerly to the day they could start fulfilling their role and start working with the oxen. Although we might think that was a small event, it was doubtless a big day for him – a stage in his rites of passage. We don't know how old he would have been but eight is a good guess since that became the English tradition, until the advent of compulsory schooling intervened in the later 19th century (the farm was the school for Early Saxon boys). That said, he would have to be older before moving on from the oxen to the plough since the design of the plough required a lad of some height in order to be able to lever its nose into the soil, not to mention the strength required. Nevertheless, each stage he passed through testified to his growing worth on the farm - a place where he'd explored every question since toddlerhood but would now stride to work with all the height and majesty of an eight year old.

The young oxen would have been quite tame, since boy and beast had grown up together, possibly sheltering under the same roof in hard weather.[14] It is highly likely that the young oxen were given lots of attention specifically to develop tameness, knowing that a close co-operative partnership would be needed in their future working lives. A few would have been hand-reared, if the cow had rejected her calf, but the ancient breeds were normally very good mothers. When the oxen reached three to fours years of age they were ready for training. Being quite tame does not mean that they wanted a yoke round their neck or the weight of a plough behind them. They had to be broken in, like any other draught animal.

Training would have started with the ox wearing a rope halter to get used to harnessing. Next it was led around till it accepted control and pace and words of command. That achieved, the oxen were paired, using a lightweight yoke, made of ash or hazel. In the sketch (*opp.*) some padding has been wrapped round for comfort, since that has been found wise by today's practitioners. It works well if the trainee ox was paired with an experienced one. Then they practised walking around as a pair, learning commands by voice and rope and the touch of the stick. Soon, a weight, such as a piece of tree, was tied on a rope attached to the yoke so that they got used to pulling. The weight could be increased until they were ready for the plough.

Finally it was time to use the full-sized, full-strength, ploughing yoke. That was bigger than you might think because it had to be long enough to span both oxen with a space between them. The preferred choice of timber in the South East was the hornbeam, with which the Saxons were familiar, for the Romano-British farmers used it too, since it had been recommended to the Romans by their top writers Vetruvius and Pliny. They knew it was the strongest timber available,[15] but was also the heaviest British timber. Indeed it was the only timber that would not split at all and so it would have defeated the normal woodworking practices of felling with an axe and then splitting timbers and planks off the trunk in the required thicknesses, by driving in wedges. Hornbeam does not co-operate with that. A yoke required being axed laboriously out of the trunk. That must have caused a lot of muttering (it's unrecorded how the Saxons swore!). No wonder they called it hardbeam rather than hornbeam. The other problem would have been the weight, for it is also the heaviest British timber[16] and so the yoke must have come as quite a surprise to the young oxen. The bows that looped round the oxen were made of ash because it produces wonderful long smooth straight rods from a coppice stool and these were not only strong enough for the job but had flexibility to 'give' with the fluctuating stress.

Once yoked, they were ready to plough. That was a morning job, an early morning job, because Saxon farmers rose in time to chase out the last nightly shadows, for the unveiling of the sun. They needed a bit of sun, for despite warmer weather there were still days when first breaths clawed the throat or when the sun crawled out with a bleary-eyed foggy hang-over. It wasn't as cheery as by the hearth where a bit of huffing and puffing had livened the embers - good to sit beside for putting on the work boots. Wet leather boots dried hard,

rasping-hard on skin over ankle bones, so feet needed wrapping. It was cheery too for the dawn meal and there'd be no other till works-end at sunset. With good bread and ale, sound boots, and a thick woollen cloak, the Saxons were ready to follow the silvering of the eastern sky. Soon the ploughman had fetched the ox-power and got the plough-nose dug in. Many of the early Saxons would have relied upon one ox. Their aim would have been to afford two, yoked together as a team and indeed called collectively 'a yoke'. The ultimate aim from the Mid Saxon period onwards, seems to have been to get eight oxen, as this became the standard unit in later documentation. Initially only the big holdings, descended perhaps from the Roman villa estates, could have shown off their power and wealth in this way. That was alright if you were not the ploughman. He had eight beasts to control, all of which had minds of their own, and of course even when paired they stretched way ahead of the plough, making the whole venture so unwieldy. Getting the team into line couldn't have been easy if any ox was new to the job. The system developed whereby experienced oxen became the front pair with the less experienced as the back pair next to the plough and new recruits sandwiched in between. If there were only two experienced oxen they became the right hand beasts of the front and back pairs. Should there be only one it went up front right and the ploughman muttered all morning. He had a partner to help urge and guide them and that was the ploughboy, until he was big enough and strong enough to handle the plough himself.

Sadly, it is not possible to sketch in words or pictures what their plough looked like. The evidence from archaeology fires heated debate and quenches no theories. The original tool was the 'ard' – a pointed digging stick drawn through the soil by the oxen and guided by the ploughman. Two designs are known from North West Europe and both were in use in Britain.[17] All they did was scratch the surface to disturb weeds and create a tilth for the seeds. They didn't break the soil beneath nor turn it over, so they did little to mix humus, aid drainage and aeration or the descent of roots to deeper levels. To scratch the surface at all thoroughly in this way meant the field had to be worked twice, at right angles to each other, and therefore fields tended to be squarish. The long narrow fields came later as a product of working an eight ox team. The ard left scars on the compacted soil beneath, which can still be found by archaeologists today. Then some design improvements were added, like having a cutting knife or coulter[18] fixed ahead of the ploughing blade or share to cut the turf and surface roots. Bracken rhizomes would have been severed easily enough but larger tree roots from out of the hedge must have brought the whole operation to an abrupt halt on many an occasion. With this extra blade added, it was easier to share deeper and the loosened soil would have shifted to either side. Somebody then had the brilliant idea of designing a mouldboard right behind the share to scoop up the loosened soil and turn it over – that created ridges and furrows that are still familiar today. Wheels were added for stability too but when exactly these improvements were introduced is a matter of heated debate.

They seem such simple ideas that it is incredible that they arrived so late. Once they were here they enabled ploughmen to move onto heavier soils and provide food for a population that was expanding again. Of course not all farmers could have afforded the latest technology and so in any one season several designs of plough could well have been seen tilthing the Surrey fields. At least we know what it was like to use one because a modern archaeologist, Francis Pryor, has tried it:-

"*I once had the doubtful pleasure of actually using an ard. It was pulled by two oxen, took all my strength and weight to keep it in the ground, and I only managed to make it penetrate about four inches deep. It was really a struggle, despite the fact that the two oxen were remarkably tame and behaved themselves excellently. I concede that ancient farmers would have had generations of skill and practice to guide them, but even so, I found it extraordinarily difficult.*"[19]

Writings like that dispel romantic notions of the lonely ploughman trudging across the landscape. How could his thoughts possibly wander into loneliness when he had to concentrate so hard! He wasn't trudging either but struggling. Similarly, the younger boys starting work as the ploughman's assistant must have had plenty upon which to concentrate in order to guide the oxen along their straight course, adjusting their pace according to the needs of the ploughman behind, fulminating over the stones and roots. In due course the boy would have taken his turn to give the ploughman's shoulders a rest until gradually he became more capable at the job, hearing less and less invective from behind. Eventually the day arrived when he was deemed a ploughman in his own right, perhaps at age twelve since that was the later tradition. Mile upon mile went into that training; ploughing furrows in the 19th century involved 10-12 miles per acre but the cutting lines of the ard were worked far closer. The mileage is unimaginable, and remember the

fields had to be worked twice each time. Only that way would they get the best tilth for the seeds and 'best' means broken evenly because the seed was not drilled in but broadcast.

These men really earned any horn of ale and crusty wholemeal bread that mum sent out to them with one of the younger children, although part of her day may well have entailed following the ard to pick stones - knobbly great flint nodules from the Downs and shards of purple ironstone from the south-western sandlands. What a weight they put in the willow-woven baskets! No wonder the women had massive muscles; much better if they had a couple of slaves. Perennial roots of noxious weeds were doubtless gathered too. Those with big tap roots, like *docce* (dock), *pistel* (thistle) and *ægwyrt* (dandelion), may have been taken home for the cooking pot. Did they realise that the pale creeping rhizomes of the couch grass were highly nutritious too ?

By now some readers will be wondering why they didn't use horses instead of oxen. Put simply, it was physically impossible. Horses and cattle are anatomically very different and so when they first tried swapping oxen for horses they found that the ox yoke constricted the windpipe of the horses and choked them. Thus horses, which had been put to work since the Iron Age, were restricted to lighter jobs. Even the ancient chariots had to be lightweight vehicles. It was not until about 700 CE[20] that they invented the rigid horse collar to take the pressure off the windpipe and onto the shoulders. That required a different means of attachment to the plough, resulting in the invention of the chains or leather straps known as 'traces'. Thereafter followed continuous argument as to which animal was best. Today's standardised 'horsepower' is 500 foot lbs per second but a real horse achieves only about 432 whereas an ox exerts approximately 288. The horse is faster but the ox is endowed with greater endurance and therefore proved more effective on heavy soils. Those were exactly what the Saxons were trying to bring into cultivation and so the ox continued to prevail. By that time the Christian Church had imposed a taboo on eating horse flesh (pagan sacred animal) and so a dead horse provided hide only, whereas a dead ox could be eaten. That made the horse more of a luxury, especially as it required special feed (oats and hay), which in turn required 'spare' land to produce them. In the 13th century Walter of Henley set out both sides of the argument which ran evenly balanced until he costed out horse-shoeing[21] and there he inflated the prices greatly, leaving the ox as the favoured draught of the plough. So the debate ran on and only in the 20th century was the last working ox team pensioned off !

That's enough about the hard slog! At the end of the day though, how did they measure their achievement? Furlongs and acres were Saxon measurements but they could not have been used in the Early Period, since 'furlong' derives from 'furrow long' and the ard did not cut furrows. That means multiplying furlongs up into acres was yet to come, along with those developments in plough technology already mentioned.

Instead, the Early Saxons must have encountered the unit used by the Romans, and still in use on the Romanised estates, and that measurement was the *iugerium*. It was about 28,000 square Roman feet or 3,000 square yards or some five eighths of an acre.[22] In simpler terms, that was reckoned to be the area that a pair of oxen could plough in a day and as such was a numerical exactitude for something that was far from exact. The term 'day' refers to what we would call a 'working day' and that was about a 'morning' with the oxen needing to be rested during the afternoon ready for work on the morrow. It sounds simple enough but there were so many variables. The morning was not measured in hours but by the stamina of the oxen, depending upon how well fed, how fit, and how experienced they were, how heavy the soil and how high the temperature, and so on. Thus the *iugerum* was more of a bureaucrat's measurement than a farmer's.

Using that unit persisted, for three reasons. Firstly, it was the established way of doing things and was therefore acceptable. Secondly, it might have been in use already with the Saxons, if the earliest migrants had arrived as soldiers to join the Roman military, and were awarded land for their services. That award would have been measured in *iugera*. After the departure of the legions the Romano-British may have also employed Germanic mercenaries who doubtless demanded the same award as those who had arrived earlier. Thirdly all these peoples were concerned over the same issue — the amount of land deemed sufficient to sustain a family at a basic level. The Germanic peoples had that notion themselves already and so the *iugerum* simply underwent a name change, to become the *hyd* (hide). Hide may seem an odd word today but its etymology reveals that crucial connection with sustaining a family. In Old Frisian *hyura* meant the members of a household, while in Old High German *hy(w)un* meant man and wife, as did *hjun* in Old Norse.[23]

The Saxon hide has proved notoriously difficult to evaluate in surface area. Later documents prove that it was just as variable as the

iugerum and so in one district a hide could be 40 acres while elsewhere it could range up to 120 acres. Textbooks say, too often, that it was 100 acres but as the OED points out, the acre itself was variable![24] Quite possibly the Saxons enlarged it as time went by because another factor came into play. As the migrants established themselves so there arose the need to pay tribute to the local bully-boy for his protection and to deter him taking their portion of land. Thus the evolution of the first kingdoms got under way. A family's land-holding needed then to be big enough, not only to sustain them, but also to pay their dues. Consequently an increase in agricultural production is detectable in the record towards the end of this Early Saxon period Their land was assessed not so much by a geometer as by a tax inspector. That makes it impossible to run our eye around a field and see it or evaluate it in the same way as did its Saxon farmers.

We can of course see some of the 'extras' in the fields that would have been noted by the Saxons. One of these would have been the lapwings,[25] for these yielded the extra seasonal bounty of eggs. Although the Saxons kept poultry, extra eggs in the spring from wild birds were always welcome. Some were sought in the cattle pastures where a number of ground-nesting birds bred, with eggs large enough to warrant collecting. Finding them was a challenge. Lapwing eggs are laid in clutches of four among tussocks, and are so highly camouflaged as to be notoriously difficult to find. Searchers would hear the emotive 'peewit' cry of the lapwings - so accusatory and yet so reproachful - drawing eyes from grass to sky. The lapwings tumbled overhead with their black and white pattern fragmenting against white clouds, confusing the eye and confounding a stooping peregrine. When searchers intruded too near their nests then with plaintive cry the lapwings dive-bombed them. No wonder the Saxons included these in their writings, with no less than three surviving instances, from the 8th and 9th centuries. The name they used is still recognisable – *læpiwince*, *læpewince*, and *lepewince* – and it is quite an exciting name because it opens a door right into the minds of the Saxons. By comparing these names with their counterparts on the Continent we find that the Heligoland Frisians used the same first syllable in their name for the hoopoe. What the two birds have in common is a crest, so we know exactly what it was about the bird that caught the Saxon eye. For confirmation there is the second syllable, *wince*, pronounced 'winch' and meant just that – something that moved up and down.[26]

Staying with the birds for a moment—another seasonal bounty was a harvest of young rooks. Up into the elms climbed the boys when the rooklets were big enough to be seen from the ground. They were more

valuable as meat than their eggs would have been, had the boys climbed earlier. Elms can be more difficult and dangerous to climb than other trees but rooking gave the boys another chance to display courage and to overtop previous achievements. It mattered not that they climbed unseen by the tiny menfolk working the fields far below, for it was the eyes of the other boys that counted. It was they who would see and pass judgement and they who would, in future years, bear that to the assembly. Good judgement by one's peers provided footholds up each man's tree of life.

Snatched rooklets were, in later times, stuffed inside the boy's shirt, ready for the descent, but Saxon costume did not lend itself to that. Probably they were pushed into a cloth sack and dropped to the gatherer grounded below. Otherwise they had their throats cut or were decapitated, releasing the blood, since blood was one of the taboo foods. Similarly, there was a taboo on consuming 'strangled' animals, ruling out wringing their necks. These taboos were ancient and were to be reinforced by the Christian Church, so on this issue there was no conflict between pagans and Christians in Early Saxon Surrey.

The rooks and crows were all part of the seasonal round of agricultural tasks that ran with the waxing and waning of the moon. Primitive or not, the ard scratching through the surface churned a few inches of good rich topsoil and it was in this that most denizens of the soil lived – the earthworms and wireworms, leatherjackets and cockchafers and all the other wrigglers and gleamers in the sight of the birds. Crows, rooks, lapwings, all learnt to follow the ard and started the veneration of this timeless image of rural life. The landscape illustrated is part of the view from the scarp of the Downs at Ranmore, albeit without the village of Westcott, which was behind the rookery and the farm was modified too. Probably the sweep of the Downs in the foreground is suggesting a more expansive open landscape than would have been the case in the early pioneer days when fields were still small and square. However, larger clearances might have been subdivided into those smaller patches and if this was done with sheep hurdles (which is highly likely), then the divisions would not necessarily show up, from this distance, at all times of the year. Similarly, the larger fields of the present-day have been subdivided with dotted lines but again might not be small enough. The aim was simply to help imaginations picture the expanse with its pattern of fields and pastures, woodlands and shaws. There would have been plenty of trees and woodlands because of the daily demand for firewood. Thus many of the trees, that look like woodland from this distance, would have been standards over-topping coppices beneath. These coppices were cropped in rotation as a renewable resource, not just for fuel but for a wealth of other products, such as the wattles from which to weave the sheep hurdles.

Into this sort of scene the Saxon plough team headed and that signalled the rooks to slip out of their rookeries in the elms to join them, with that great cawing clamour of theirs. It was the cawing that is thought to have given rise to the name ‘rook’ in imitation. It comes from the Saxon *hroc* but is similar in neighbouring languages, enabling Saxons to understand travellers from over the North Sea.[27] The same can be said for the crows, called by the Saxons *crawan*.[28] The bones of both have been identified from the rubbish heaps of Saxon Southampton, still bearing the cut marks where the meat was knifed off the bone.[29] Perhaps, therefore, we should imagine the

plough team being joined by village boys armed with their sling-shots. Otherwise they climbed the elms and took the large rooklets from the nests.[30]

Watching the birds has diverted our attention. Let us look back at the cattle again and look more closely at their guardians, the oxherd and the cowherd. They had two duties. One was to stop the livestock wandering off across the open pastures and the other was to safeguard them from wolves and rustlers.

Cows in lactation are more likely to be nearest the farmsteads for ease of milking. Who did the milking I have not been able to ascertain with any certainty. By Tudor times it was the men who went out and milked the cows in the fields and brought the milk back to the women on dairy duty. In Saxon times, however, there does not seem to have been such a clear division of duty so there is freedom to imagine women doing this. It would be logical for the head woman to stay at the farm, supervising the daily round, while slaves and underlings were dispatched out to the cows.

The guardians could just as easily have been women but it would seem from later written references that this was most often a man's job. This sexist division of labour might not be as stereotypical as it appears, for there may have been religious connotations. Possibly it was a man's job if some of their deities of protection were for men only. Those associated with the boar would be high contenders but we do not know. Doubtless they took some comfort from feeling that the gods were looking after them amid the lupine howlings of remote dark nights. How cold it must have been; especially out on the grasslands of Horley next to Gatwick which was so often the coldest place in the South East. Part of the day's work must have been to cut firewood and return it to camp, using an ox as a pack animal. That suggests they worked in pairs: one on day duty, one on night duty, even though later references imply a lonesome job. The oxherd on night duty could be quite some distance from his sleeping partner back at base camp, so it *would* have felt a lonesome job. Even if the camp was away to the side in the sheltering woods, near the fuel supply, the herd and its night watchman would be well out on the grazings. That way wolves and rustlers[31] had to emerge from cover. Their greatest fears were the dogs.

Just as shepherds had sheep dogs, so oxherds had cattle dogs. They were of two main types, rather than two breeds. The notion of a 'breed' that is visually recognisable is largely a 19th century development. Before that, for thousands of years, dogs were not judged on their looks but on their deeds. Desired characteristics, like fierceness, stamina, speed, grip etc. were bred selectively for fulfilling a range of needs. Cattle dogs needed to be inherently loyal, possessive, fierce, alert and speedy. That gave rise to a sort of 'greyhound' crossed with the big hunting dog of the times (think deerhound) and was their version of a 'lurcher'. Probably many were rough coated but an illustration from late Saxon times[32] is smooth like a greyhound except for a rough tail. The look of a greyhound is an ancient look, very similar to the cattle dogs on a Saharan rock painting from 2000 BCE.[33] Such dogs knew how to see off anything and it has been suggested that I should draw them with large leather collars to protect them from wolves biting their throats. The Late Saxon illustration certainly shows such a collar. These dogs allowed the oxherd some sleep, in the knowledge that anything untoward would set the dogs baying and wake him up.

When it came to moving the herd they needed the second type of dog. These were 'driving' dogs or 'heelers' because they nipped the heels of the cattle to make them move. They had to be small, in the sense of short-legged, and have a natural inclination to flatten themselves on the ground following a nip. That saved them from injury if the hoof was lashed out. It went over their heads. We have a very good idea of what those dogs looked like because the last of the English heelers, the Lancashire Heeler,[34] has been saved from extinction. There is also the Welsh bloodline, of the Cardigan Corgi (as opposed to the Pembroke Corgi), which is often said to have been brought into West Wales much later by the Vikings. However, we know that the *type* is ancient.[35] There's a beautiful painting of one

in an Egyptian tomb, showing it smooth coated, with longish thin tail and long pointed snout.[36] They had been brought right across Europe far earlier by the Celtic peoples and it is from their language that we get the name Corgi, meaning small dog.[37] They were variable, in terms of exact size, length of tail, roughness of coat, but nevertheless had that distinctive Corgi look about them, particularly the way their front feet turn outwards. It was of course their character not their looks that counted and having been hunting dogs it was their bravery and ferocity that was kept in the bloodline; no rustler, wolf or fractious bull deterred a Corgi.

Even doing the quick sketches of corgi-type dogs gives time to think. How, for example, was this system managed? In particular, who owned the dogs? At first my mind went along the lines that individual households kept a cattle dog, whether Corgi or lurcher, which they passed on to the oxherd along with the cattle, rather than the oxherd maintaining a pack of dogs himself.[38] Then I realised that a dog serves but one master. They must have belonged to the oxherd. His loyalty to the herd and his dedication to duty were secured by him being paid out of the return from the cattle. Those payments must have included meat for the dogs.

In many places their work would have been divided into two seasons as per their calendar. During the long 'winter' season all could be seen together, adjacent to the farmstead homes, where the livestock were returned each night. It is easy to imagine them dotted along the lengthy green at Dunsfold with the line of homes down one side, or gathered around one of its little ponds for drinking. Each morning they were driven out to pastures further away and returned each evening. Between times the homesteaders nipped out to gather the cow-pats for fuel and fertilizer. As the year rolled into longer days and longer grass so it was time to move out to the summer pastures, often miles away.[39] This transhumance agriculture gave rise to summertime communities, some of which developed into permanent villages out in the Weald. In the south of Surrey is Oakwood, which is still just a church in a wood amid the pastures. Although what stands today dates from the 13th century, getting to this one spot by a pathway through the trees, down a deep gully, crossing the brook, and up the steep

climb out of the gully into the grassy space of the churchyard, focuses the mind sharply as to what the remote isolated communities were like. Calling them communities implies more than just the oxherds and in all likelihood the wives and children went too. It was crucial to take the youngsters so that they would learn the route and the boundaries. Such a system was still operating as recently as the Edwardian period, in countries like Norway, where whole families moved up the mountains to the summer pastures with their cattle.

It is not clear whether we should imagine the oxherd and his family trudging off with a few cattle or whether this was a combined operation with other neighbouring farms, resulting in a cattle drove. If the system evolved into the latter they needed a planning meeting. There were no pubs so they met in the home or 'hall' of the group leader. His leadership status had to be earned and then maintained, in their hierarchical society. Where a family grouping of homes made up a farmstead the leader was most likely the founder, providing he was still fit enough, but if farmsteads worked in conjunction with each other for the drove then an overall leader needed electing. The gathering looked for both wisdom and the grace to acknowledge that of others, plus acumen in farming and business. Above all, he must be a good warrior or, if untested, show convincing aptitude for defending the herd. This was all judged by the men of the hall and they would depose the inadequate. That sounds fine but anybody who has sat on a committee will foresee problems. Their way of overcoming them leaves us aghast. With the hall becoming the pub, they all downed enough ale or mead to loosen their tongues. That way their speech was truthful. Nobody's reputation was safe. Out went etiquette and diplomacy. Out came fists and knives and on occasions, at really crucial councils, souls departed for the Other World. What a way to run their business – but – here comes the clever bit. They then slept on their decisions and when sober the next day they reviewed what had been said so freely and arrived at the best judgement.[4] Cattle droves were a chance for the younger members to start taking responsibility and begin earning their place in society; this was when it mattered who had shown the greatest bravery climbing the highest elms to get the rooklets.

It is to be hoped that the business of organising a drove was dispensed with quickly and safely as a matter of routine without bloodshed but we do get an insight into councils concerning weighty 'matters of state' over defence of their lands in times of trouble. Such war meetings obviously required representation from over a much wider area and so we see how the Saxon war leaders, like Aella beaching his warband on the south coast to found Sussex, came to the fore and had to maintain superiority. From this, strong tribal leadership led to kingship once early Saxon kingdoms became established, during the period we are considering.

Thus if we picture the farmsteads dotted across the landscape of South East England we should not view them as 'isolated'. They were part of an unseen network, linked by obligations. One of those obligations was to host their foremost leader as he travelled around his district reminding people that their land and their protection were ultimately due to him, provided that they paid their 'protection money'. Credit was not part of the deal.

Such a visitation could drain a farm's resources rapidly and so two expedients came into play. One was that farms became grouped in order to share responsibility for the provisioning. The second was an agreement that no visitation would last longer than three days.[41] Thus a group of farms organising a drove were in fact working part of a much larger system and one where the oxherds attendant at the summer pastures held responsibilities beyond the immediate communities back home.

END NOTES

1 They just needed enough surplus to trade for commodities that they did not produce themselves, although as they became established they also developed an eye for luxury goods, such as fine cloth richly dyed and the brooches with which to fasten it. The Jutes to the east, in Kent, especially eastern Kent, were far keener on self-display than were the Saxons in what became Surrey. The kingdom of Kent was split, for royal administration, into east and west, and this may be significant in terms of these cultural differences. See Yorke.

2 The use of 'breed' does not occur until the mid 16th century.

3 I am grateful to the Weald and Downland Museum for the loan of their oxen photographs and for their permission to draw from them, for some of the illustrations.

4 Info. courtesy of Mr. Sid Pennington of Pondtail Farm, Cobham, Surrey now retired.

5 Place-names of Surrey p.42.

6 Recorded in 675, albeit in a 13th century copy that might not be accurate. Place-names of Surrey p.42.

7 De Cleene and Lejeune, p.295.

8 Graves, Robert (1960); The Greek Myths; vol.1, pp.51-2; Penguin Books.

9 The ancient Greeks explained this with the myth that Eris (blackthorn) caused strife for her twin brother Ares (hawthorn) and the two should never be left on their own together; Robert Graves, The Greek Myths; vol.1, pp.51-2; Penguin Books.

10 See Lockwood.

11 See Gavin Smith for example.

12 Hagen 1995, p.142.

13 Info. ref. cranes courtesy of Ian Peters at RSPB HQ. Other places named after cranes include Cranborne, Dorset; Cranbourne, Hants; Cornwell, Oxon and Cranwell, Lincs; from Gelling and Cole p.12. An alternative Saxon name, trani gives Tranwell, Northumberland; Gelling and Cole p.32. The 'leigh' for 'clearing' could be spelt 'ley', as was Cranleigh till changed in the 20thC. by the Post Office. The cranes stood at about 120cm and so *did* get a good view over the bovine backs.

14 Cattle byres have not been found for the early period but the climate was warmer and so perhaps they were not needed.

15 Hornbeam has a strength of 17.7 Newtons/ mm^2; Oak has only 14.5.

16 Hornbeam 51 lb per cubic foot; Oak 46-52 lb. More details in Howkins and Sampson.

17 See Brigden. The two types, the bow ard and the crook ard are illustrated p.6. My illustration is of the bow ard type, believed to be the commonest.

18 They called it a *culter*, hence today's coulter. Share from Saxon *scearu* meaning cutting or division, becoming a military term for a division of their troops but was retained as a plough term.

19 Pryor ; 2006; p.66.

20 Urquart p.116.

21 Horse-shoeing had been invented by the Romans for their hard road surfaces (time of Valentinian 375-92 CE).

22 Approximately 28,000 square Roman feet or 3,000 square yards.

23 Support for this notion of a unit capable of sustaining a family crops up again later when Saxon written records specify that slaves given their freedom (in terms of rights but still owing obligations and labour services to their lord) had to be given the use of a piece of land large enough to support them, and that allotment was just this size being discussed.

24 Acre defined by OED as area of land one chain (four rods) in width by one furlong in length. As the traditional furlong could vary in length from country to country, so did the acre. In England an acre was 4,840 square yards, in Scotland 6,150 square yards and in Ireland 7,840 square yards. It is a Saxon unit, meaning field. Probably meant to be

"as much area as could be plowed in one day".

25 Lapwing eggs were gathered for sale right into the later 20th century. It is a very Germanic thing to do and even today in Holland, where the bird is considered 'very Dutch', the first egg of the year is presented to the Queen of the Netherlands.

26 From Lockwood, p.93.

27 Old High German *hruoh*; Dutch *roek*; Old Norse *hrokr*. Lockwood p.131.

28 Crow etymology Lockwood p.49.

29 Hagen; 1995, p.143.

30 This practice is still remembered, for rook pies, from places like Limpsfield. On the whole, the great rookeries have disappeared from Surrey, along with the elms, following Dutch Elm Disease from 1970 onwards.

31 See Pryor 2003.

32 Illus. for September in the Julius Work Calendar; Cotton MS Julius A.VI; British Library.

33 At Sefar. Reproduced p.4 Hancock.

34 See Hancock p.17; includes photos.

35 Teckel (or Tessem) family, which includes Bassets and Dachshunds.

36 Tomb at Beni-Hassan; XII Dynasty; c.2000 BCE. Shown on http://www.wits-end-ranch.com/page3.html.

37 Not all authorities agree with this translation; the etymology engenders debate.

38 The value of such a dog was equal to that of an ox in the early Welsh laws.

39 I'm not convinced they waited until May to start the transhumance. Many communities could well have been running short of grazing before then and they needed to give ample chance for the home pastures to run up to flower ready for the vital hay harvest. However, it is possible suckling cows and their calves remained behind. The return from summer pastures would have been signalled by the sun rolling down towards the autumn equinox because thereafter the declining light intensity triggered hormones that brought the cattle into readiness for mating. The livestock must have been reunited for that in order to select the best for the breeding programme.

40 For an extended review of this see Pollington 2003.

41 More details in Hagen 1995 and Pollington 2003.

***

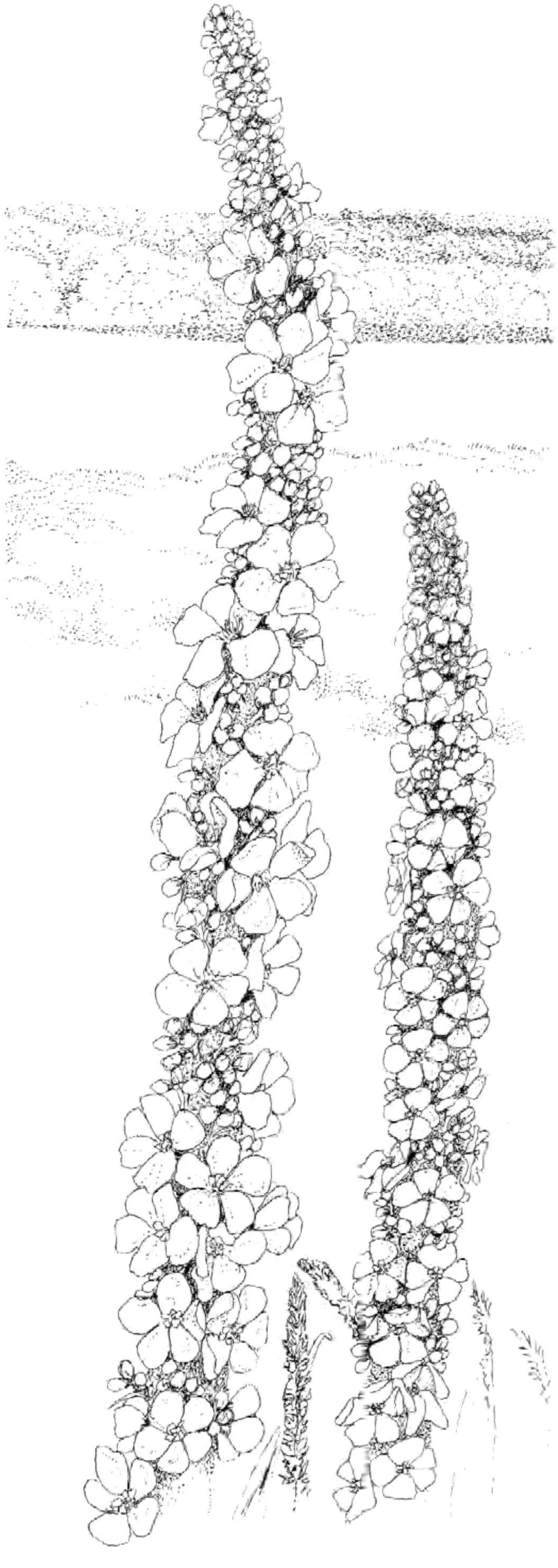

Great Mullein (right) also known as Bullocks Lungwort is a reminder of vetinary herbalism but how this was employed by the Early Saxons is unknown, since so few clues came through into the written record. we know practically nothing of early Saxon practice.

SHEEP, SHEPHERDS AND WOLVES

In our imaginations, let us return again to the Early Saxon landscape, where the upper Wey watered itself a green ribbon of meadows through the muted heathlands at Elstead. It would have been prime sheep country. Out in the heather ranged flocks of several hundred, with fleeces of duns and roans, greys and browns and black, admixtured with white, all blended beautifully in the dappled shadows under birches when they rested from the sun.

Since the end of the spring the flocks would have been moved out from the riverside pastures so as to leave the meadow grasses and wild flowers to bolt up to bloom ready for the hay harvest. We can imagine a good hay year, with it cut and dried and ricked into conical insurances against the meanness of the next winter and then an after-thought of rain would have greened up the beige aftermath with fresh eddish.[1] Then the sheep would have been brought back for a good feed before shearing – good feed grew good fleeces; poorer feed grew fleeces with weaker fibres, still embodied in the Saxon textiles. A fragment of woollen cloth entwines an astonishment of unexpected detail.[2]

The Romans, it is thought, introduced new bloodstock with a white fleece, which could be dyed bright colours. That made it very desirable so no wonder the bloodline was perpetuated into Saxon times since they loved colour too. Curiously their relatives back on the Continent gave up Roman sheep[3] and reverted to the natural duns and browns and blacks of the more primitive breeds. These had devolved from the vari-coloured sheep of the Iron Age plus a brown-fleeced breed of the Soay type (illus. p.68). The Soay bones show up distinctly in the archaeological record because of their peculiar pelvis design, which made them a popular breed by facilitating easy lambing. The Soay type were short-tailed but when crossed with the Roman they got long tails.[4] That cross produced particularly good sheep and so their descendants are still farmed today; the closest is said to be the Norfolk Horned breed (*opening illus.*).[5]

Saxon sheep skulls found by archaeologists show that both rams and ewes were horned, although some strains had hornless ewes while further strains were polled. All these skeletal and colour variations being interbred must have made a very mixed flock indeed. Nevertheless, the fact that the white Roman breed can be detected in the record for so long implies there were specialist farms with pedigree flocks. Doubtless such flocks were raised within fairly easy reach of prime markets where the fleeces would attract the highest valuations (rather than being for home/ local use) and so might well have been seen on a walk through the meadows of Elstead. Nearer to London and other Thames-side settlements would probably have been where mixed flocks were being reared, primarily for meat and milk, which needed prompt marketing.

Sheep destined for meat were taken into the markets alive and so we need to imagine small numbers on the move through the lanes across the landscape. Many of these routes must have been of ancient usage, going back through the Roman period and into the Iron Age. Some have become the roads of today, such as 'The Maultway' (the B3015) at Camberley, identified as a link in a chain of ancient trackways relating to the Blackwater Valley. Its name is believed to derive from the Celtic *mollt* for sheep.[6]

How the traffic on these routes was organised to ensure regular supplies of fresh food in the developing Saxon centres such as *Lundenwic* is unknown. The Saxons would have taken over the pre-existing system that supplied Roman London from the hinterland but it still took administrative skills to run it. Although our attention is focussed upon farming we should not get blinkered to the wider picture and forget those who proved themselves able administrators. The speed with which the new kingdoms were forged speaks volumes.

On arrival at market centres the sheep needed holding areas nearby and so fields must have been set-aside specifically for this purpose. The best known, and one of Saxon usage, is London's Smithfield. Maybe there was a hay rick or two by the side for feed since we have no idea how long the sheep had to wait but neither do we know whether it mattered to the Saxons how long the livestock were kept without food. What we do know, from the skeletal evidence, is that in the long term, the flocks were healthy and well-managed, except in drought years when grazing was at a premium. From the Welsh laws we know they had similar health problems to those of today, from rot, scab and red water to mange. These problems were recognised and taken seriously, with penalties for trading afflicted sheep. In the case of mange the sheep were not allowed on the site again for seven years.[7]

Returning to our walk, imagine it was about the beginning of July. The sheep would have been due for shearing, as though the hay-making hadn't been work enough. By then the ewes would have been fattening up again after lambing and the fine-ended fleeces of Soay type sheep would have been thickening. It is conjectural whether sheep were washed prior to shearing but at some date the practice evolved. Around Elstead they would have used a side-stream of the Wey, normally the crystal palace of the kingfisher,[8] and dammed it temporarily with wattle hurdles to back up an extra depth of water. Therein, they had a stony bed for a firm footing while they worked on any fleeces caked with dung, giving them a brisking with a bunch of birch twigs. This would have been important for white sheep although even these would not need much washing since the sandy soils of the heath are clean soils, not leaving the fleeces cemented with clay. The stony stream would not have choked with staining mud either. Even so, a quick dip and a rub round the rear would not have gone amiss.[9] It is tempting to guess that getting into the water was reserved for slaves and presumably there were no gender differences. Women worked as shepherds[10] and since they were in fine muscle after the hay-making there was no problem over pitching a wayward sheep into the stream.

Shearing was a necessity because the wool grew continuously. The days when primitive sheep had an annual moult that could be plucked were long gone. Shears are commonly found, and very variable, but the largest, with pointed blades and looped handles, are considered to be for sheep-shearing rather than trimming beards. With the most powerful farmers having several hundred sheep to shear we can doubtless presume that speed was of the essence and that shearers worked competitively, rivalling each other as to how many they could shear in a day, and thereby enhance their reputations. Choosing this time of the year meant that not only had the fleece thickened up again but fresh yellow lanolin had risen from the skin, and the art was to shear just above this clear yellow level, so that the lanolin lubricated the shears and cooled the blades, increasing speed of shearing. The lanolin was left behind to waterproof the sheep till more fleece grew.[11] Whether the setting was at the farmstead or out on the pastures we do not know but if the former then we can be sure it was all observed critically by a whole cluckery of chickens.

Counting sheep puts us to sleep. Learning to count is a different matter. Saxon mothers doubtless taught their little children, just as mothers do today, and with only slight changes in the spellings, as in the numbers one to ten:- *an*, *twegen*, *thri*, *feower*, *fif*, *sex*, *seofon*, *eahta*, *nigon*, *tien*. Now, having said that, an anomaly appears in the alternative ways of counting sheep that existed around the regions until recently.[12] These used numerals in what the general reader would call regional dialects. Instead of showing descent from various Old English (Saxon) languages, these came from the British (Celtic) languages. They have a rhythmic rhyming structure which you can hear if you chant this Suffolk version out loud: *ina*, *mina*, *tethera*, *methera*, *pin*, *sithera*, *lithera*, *cothera*, *hothra*, *dik*.[13] You may have to try chanting that a second time to get the full swing of it! The numerals work in pairs up to five and then again up to ten.

There are regional variations to this pattern so if a Surrey Saxon went trading over the border he would hear the South Saxons counting: *ein*, *tein*, *tuthera*, *futhera*, *fim*, *shavera*, *lackera*, *ko*, *debera*, *dik*. Notice the

change at eight and nine. Although there were differences in some of the numerals it would be possible to trade from region to region, using finger signs if need be, with all the systems in England being denary (base ten; decimal).

It becomes even more intriguing when linguists start explaining that the numerals are expressed in the female gender and therefore likely to have been used for counting ewes (and must have included wethers; castrates). Several historians conclude that sheep must have been counted in pairs but I could not find a debate on the practical implications of this - when a Saxon traded 50 sheep were 100 animals involved? The survival of British counting systems (when precious few other British words survived) has enormous implications, albeit seen through such a tiny window. To many historians it implies that migrant Saxons conquered the British and relegated them to the lowliest jobs, like being a shepherd. That idea derives from later writings (primarily of Gildas).

The Suffolk example beginning with *ina, mina*.....may remind some readers of the children's counting-out chant beginning *eeny, meeny, mina, mo*. That too has engendered a lot of debate as to its age. The wording in the versions known today seems to be modern[14] but obviously draws inspiration from the old.[15] It is all too easy to dismiss material from childhood as just kids' stuff but that misses a crucial point. A lot of ancient material is trapped in the world of childhood simply because children do not update it (except to make jokes topical). Children always strive to reach the next stage in their growing up, longing to do things that older or bigger children do, and so when they deem themselves to have outgrown something they do not bother to change it but simply stalk off, leaving it behind as little kids' stuff. Thus the lore of childhood has preserved material relating to the Celtic measurement of time in nights rather than days. For example, the practical jokes on April Fool's Day must end at noon. Boys pushing girls into the nettles on Ascension Day must stop at noon. Boys punching boys who cannot produce an oak leaf on St. George's Day must stop at noon. Why noon? Many texts say 'origin lost' or something similar but it makes perfect sense if time was originally measured in nights as opposed to days. The 24 hours would have to run from midday to midday instead of the current midnight to midnight. Thus the rising sun brought in a new day that would be 'today' only till noon and then in effect the afternoon would become 'tomorrow'. The rest of the 'today' had been the afternoon and evening of 'yesterday'. This actually made sound practical sense because a sacred 'day' would be split into two periods of ritual,

allowing for essential livestock management during the other hours.[16] Our pagan Early Saxons kept this system as they converted to Christianity, with the pre-Reformation Church being entirely so timetabled with each sacred saint's day being styled the Eve of the Feast Day of …followed by the Feast Day of… Some of the system survived the Reformation and so we still have Christmas Eve, New Year's Eve, Midsummer's Eve, Twelfth Night, etc. plus that redundant relic, the 'fortnight' from fourteen nights. It's amazing what echoes can still be heard.[17]

Whatever counting system was used, it must have been such a relief when the last sheep was sheared. Can't you just hear the groans of the shearers straightening their backs! How gaunt and skinny the sheep looked without their fleeces. What a relief though to watch them being shepherded away by the eager sheepdogs. Again there were big fierce dogs for defence, as per those needed by the oxherd (think of German Shepherd Dogs), and then the controlling dogs bred to keep their natural pack-animal traits for rounding up. The latter have devolved into today's collies and so to imagine collie dogs in Early Saxon Surrey is probably right. That is the type I have drawn but it was the Victorians who standardised their appearance. It was the inherent herding instincts that singled out collie-type dogs from other working dogs and permitted the 'Border Collie' to rise through the social ranks of Victorian dog-ownership where other farm dogs were considered too low-class.

The name 'collie' had secured its place by 1875 but is believed to be ancient although there are at least five arguments as to what it means. One line stems from the Gaelic word for 'useful', with the word for dog being *co* (pronounced koh). A second line has it deriving from the Welsh *coelius* for loyal. A third relates it to the colley breed of Scottish sheep and therefore it was originally a 'colley dog'. The fourth relates it to a German sheepdog called 'Alt Deutscher Kuli' where

Illus. left: Soay type sheep

kuli means worker, probably from the Latin *collaborare* meaning to collaborate and could have been picked up by the Saxons from over the Roman frontier of the homelands. Finally, it could come from ancient words for black, meaning the dog that worked the black-faced sheep, hence 'collie dog' meaning sheep dog. Thus black-faced miners are 'colliers', hewing the 'coal'. These col/black words are ancient, cropping up in some form or other in nearly all the languages of North West Europe, so the Saxons would have understood the British shepherds on this point and it was the ancestors of the British who are thought to have brought the basic breed of dog to the country sometime between the 5th and 1st centuries BCE. Then the Romans improved the strain to give us something closer to today's idea of a collie. Remember appearances did not matter – it was that herding instinct that counted, and more significantly, the way these dogs watched the shepherd so that once trained they could be operated by eye-contact and hand-signals. If the word does indeed come from the British languages then it could be seen as further evidence that the Saxons relegated the British to slavery and low status jobs like shepherding.

After shearing, the next concern was the less strenuous overseeing of the rams tupping their ewes but that was not until well into the autumn. When the roar of rutting stags disturbed the peace then the rams got active too.[18] It was the natural way of things, to ensure the young are not born during the leanest weeks of the new year. Gestation for the Soay types, for example, was about five months,[19] which took lambing well into the spring. This was important because the developing lamb took up room inside the ewe, so reducing the amount her stomach could hold, at just the time when she needed most feed.[20] The size of the unborn lamb increases significantly during the last month of gestation. Therefore quality needed to compensate for reduced quantity. Poor winter pasture, hay and heather were not always good enough; she needed the richer nutrition from the burgeoning of spring. Sheep high up on the Hindhead hills would have been brought down to the lower heaths around Thursley when the weather was harshest and then moved on to the Wey meadows towards Elstead at springburst; a system that was repeated right across Surrey heathlands, to Limpsfield Chart in the east.

It also meant the sheep were brought out of the wilder parts and closer to the farmsteads where they were safer from wolves. How many wolves there were in Surrey we have no idea but there were plenty in Saxon minds.[21] It was their image of the fearful and of evil, persisting into the later Saxon literature and indeed the literature throughout North West Europe.[22] Despite their notoriety they occur in surprisingly few place-names in the whole country and none in Surrey.[23] However, we would be right to imagine wolf packs sweeping these Elstead/Thursley heaths from their retreats up in the Hindhead hills to the south because there is a reference to them in the bounds of the Bishop of Winchester's manor of Farnham. The route described ran up through the Devil's Punch Bowl - *on gerihtne to wulf horan* – straight to wolf slope.[24] Anyone who has been engulfed in the depths of the mist-choked Punch Bowl will have no difficulty imagining the howling of the wolves! Obviously the wolf slope was a well-known local landmark but for it to be a suitable habitat for wolves required woodland and so we should not imagine all the Hindhead hills[25] cleared of trees to create heather pasture for sheep. That was the case lower down though, for at Thursley the boundary passes through *crudan sceat* where *sceat* refers to sheep.[26] No doubt the shepherds felt much threatened by the wolves since it is difficult to imagine there was much for them to prey upon; rabbits[27] and fallow deer[28] were yet to be introduced and even rats were still a rarity, restricted more or less to ports like Southampton, London and York.[29] Their largest prey would have been red deer and then roe deer, the bones of which occur in the butchers' waste in places like *Hamwic* (Southampton), testifying to their local availability. There are far more remains of red deer than roe but that may not reflect local populations since hunters would have sought out the red rather than the roe because it gave a bigger return. Deer are not easy prey though and by the time of the written records venison seems to have been a fairly scarce meat[30] and probably for the elite rather than the lower ranks.[31] However, when times were hard and opportunity availed itself, venison was doubtless in many a lowly cooking pot!

Frequently the wolves must have been hunting much smaller prey such as hares, which again put them into conflict with people since hare was desirable for the cooking pot and was also a sacred animal.[32] By later Saxon times hares were being conserved for the elite as was the meat of beavers (tails a separate delicacy). Beavers were not extinct yet. Their bones were found in the butchers' waste at West Stow[33] and their teeth turn up in graves to the end of this pagan period,[34] while in the South East they gave their name to the Beverley Brook that flows into the Thames at Battersea.[35] Not only were they hunted for meat but also for their fur and that was highly valued – worth 120 pence in the Welsh Laws when the value of the king's harp was the same and a wolf pelt was worth a mere eight pence.

The famous lyre from the Sutton Hoo ship burial was in a beaver-skin bag.[36]

On the whole, the wolves themselves seemed to have escaped the cooking pot, judging by their absence from the butchers' waste heaps. That, however, implies that in communities such as *Hamwic* (Southampton), the meat did not have a trade value. Out in the countryside wolves might have been eaten as an added benefit from successful pest control. Certainly wolf meat is prescribed as wholesome for the sick in later medical treatise,[37] implying knowledge gained from experience. Equally certain was the need for pest control seeing as a wolf needs about 3.6kg of meat per day,[38] hence the references to pit traps as boundary markers in the later charters. The bleating of new-born lambs would have attracted hungry packs from far away. Maybe that was a contributing factor to the sharp decline in Scots Pine on the heathlands, which is attributed usually to grazing pressure but could indicate cutting and drying for a precautionary heap by the lambing folds which would burn furiously, with intense heat, light and crackling, if fired to drive off wolves

It would certainly have lit up the early spring night in dark valleys where the ewes were enfolded. These gave some protection from the easterlies off the March heathlands and the nearby farmstead was a bit of a deterrent to the wolves. There was drinking water too, if needed, but the ewes took surprisingly little. Mainly it was convenient for the shepherds, working their shifts alongside the sun and the moon, watching the ewes for signs of imminent birth and signs of stress. All were pointed out to the next generation of youngsters. The scream of a vixen distracted them, the howls of the wolves disturbed them, but lambing proceeded as relentlessly as the splitting of buds on the birch trees. Fortunately the old breeds were blessed with easy births but there was always a risk of problems, as when on rare occasions a ewe would reject her lamb, which then had to be whisked to the warming fireside and hand-reared on horns of milk. The younger children loved that job. They loved the way plain sheep would have spotty lambs and then wondered where the spots went.[39] Few lambs were eaten at this period. They were matured as a valued source of milk and wool and only at the end of their productive lives were they culled.[40] However joints of lamb occasionally surface as grave goods to feed the soul on its journey to the Other World. I did smile on reading that somebody at Burwell, Cambs., was sent off to the Otherworld with a meal of lamb chops![41]

Fleeces were probably bundled up in cloth as per today. These could then be stowed at home. Excavations have revealed that the homes had a sunken 'cellar' under the floor which has caused much debate, with a popular suggestion being that these were for storage. This seemed perfectly feasible when demonstrated to us at the reconstructed site at West Stow. It solved the problem of the soot, from the open fire, that coated everything in the room above. The warm air carried the soot upwards leaving the underfloor cavity clean and suited to storing fleeces, out of season clothing etc. This construction is known as 'grubenhausen'.

END NOTES

1 Surrey dialect word for the fresh aftergrowth which, in common with some other local terms, is straight from the Saxon.

2 Weak fibres from poor feed are known today as 'weak staple' and producers are penalised by the wool graders. For detail of the different types/ grades of Early Saxon fleece see Walton Rogers. Interestingly, the fabric remains from Hamwic (Southampton) have these weak fibres so perhaps the sheep lived on the heathlands that would become part of the New Forest.

3 See Rogers p.13.

4 Tails are docked nowadays to save sheep from maggot infestation but ancient breeds were troubled rarely with this.

5 Permission to draw and information from Kerry Long, www.norfolkhornsheep.co.uk/ .

The modern version is about 20lb heavier than the Saxon (Hagen 1995, p.85).

6 See George Poulter, The History of Camberley, 1937, pp. 3-4. Thanks to Sharon Cross, Surrey Heath Museum, for assistance with this.

7 From Hagen 1995, p.87.

8 Kingfishers (*illus. right)* were known simply as fiscere by c.1000 but earlier it was isen or isern, meaning iron-coloured, after its metallic sheen. The bird is less than two inches longer than a robin. In Saxon times the robin was probably a scarce woodland bird, as it is still in much of Europe.

9 Sheep-washing is conjectural based upon probability; no archaeological evidence traced. Washing white fleeces was to try to increase their market value.

10 Women shepherds conjectural, based upon

references later in the Middle Ages but as there was probably a shortage of labour on some Early Saxon farms women presumably did some of the shepherding.

11 The lanolin layer is known as the yolk in most counties, after its egg colour. Info. from Norfolk shepherd working Soay. Pers. Comm. Grace Corne.

Modern electric shearing goes beneath the yolk. Pers. Comm.. John Worsfold

12 A version recorded in Sussex as late as 1957.

13 See BARRY, M (1964) "Traditional Enumeration in the North Country" in *Folk Life* 7, 75-91.

14 19th century, with the earliest written versions thought to be 1855. That is when they started to be popularised and would not reflect, in all cases, the date of origin. Some versions that include the word 'nigger' are presumed to be of American origin, and one of these was popularised by Rudyard Kipling in Land and Sea Tales for Scouts and Guides, in 1923.

15 Another indication of antiquity lies in the versions that can be found in other European languages and in India.

16 We do not know what taboos existed about working on the sacred days in the Northern European cultures. From the Middle East we are familiar with the Judaic law of keeping the Sabbath holy, which then passed into Christianity although even in the New Testament there is debate about interpretation, with Jesus being challenged upon this issue - see Luke 14, 1-6 and Matthew 12, 1-13. The taboo on working on a Sunday in England is largely Victorian interpretation. With thanks to Revd Barry North for assistance on this.

17 Similarly, eating lamb to celebrate Midsummer persists in many parts of Europe and so we ought to imagine this as part of the sheep-rearing year.

18 Due to changing levels of light intensity affecting hormones in the brain.

19 Specifically 147-155 days for today's Soay.

20 This is particularly crucial during the last month of gestation when the unborn lamb increases its weight significantly.

21 Last wolf killed in England was reputedly in 1500 and well over a century later in Scotland.

22 The best-known today would be Fenrir, the wolf son of the god Loki in Norse mythology and the wolves in Little Red Riding Hood and The Three Little Pigs.

23 See Yalden.

24 Some people (see Gelling) believe Hindhead takes its name from the red deer hinds and that would support the theory that large amounts of woodland could still be found thereabouts.

25 From Gover et al. p.185 From other parts of England we find wolf evidence in boundary charters featuring wulsathe and wulpitte for a wolf pit (where wolves were lured and trapped) and by wulfhaga for a wolf-hedge to protect a fold.

26 Site located at Thursley's cricket ground.

27 Introduced by the Normans; Yalden p.158.

28 It is arguable whether Fallow Deer were a Roman or a Norman introduction. Lever believes in a Roman date and cites Saxon references but Hagen (1995; p.134) disputes his translations although concedes that a bone fragment from Cheddar was identified as Fallow. Yalden p.152 concurs with Hagen.

29 These were Black Rats, a Roman introduction, Yalden 125. Brown Rats did not arrive until 18thC. Yalden 183.

30 Hagen 1992, p.72.

31 Hagen 1992, p.145.

32 The original 'Easter bunny'.

33 Hagen 1995, p.132.

34 Hagen 1995, p.362.

35 Gover et al, p.2.

36 See Hagen 1992, p.104.

37 The pelt on the other hand would have warmed a Saxon as much as the wolf but sadly Walton Rogers does not include furs in her survey.

38 Yalden p.270.

39 Kerry Long reported, 'Most of the lambs are spotty – or else completely black. They have passed this characteristic on to the Suffolk breed.'

Black sheep are culled today because the wool cannot be dyed and there is but a limited demand for the natural black, from craft weavers etc.

40 Conclusion based upon the archaeological evidence although sites vary; at Portchester, Hants. Early to Mid period evidence includes lambs eaten at six months onwards. The documentary evidence, which all comes from the later periods, shows the Saxons had by then developed a taste for lamb meat and it was common since the Saxons like fatty meat (extra calories) and it was unsaturated fat, unlike today's.

41 See WILKINSON, M. (1986); *Withowinde*; LXXVII, 16.

HEROIC WEED

And you, waybread mother of plants,
Open to the east, mighty within,
Carts ran over you, ladies rode over you,
Brides cried over you, bulls snorted over you,
You withstood all then, and you were crushed,
So may you withstand poison and infection,
And the evil that travels round the land.

(Pollington, 2000,p.215)

Waybread in the text above is the broad-leaved plantain, cursed by gardeners today when it flattens its rosettes into the lawn. What is now a weed in Britain is a valuable herb cultivated for medicines in the Ukraine, while to the Early Saxons it was sacred. Weed or not, it will serve well for reminding modern readers that all the landscape was sacred to the Saxons but not viewed dourly as heavy theology. The faith was spread orally and was therefore rich in memorable, entertaining stories and folk songs, most of which are lost to us today but we do get a glimpse by way of the plantain.

The extract above is from the Late Saxon herbal known as the *Lacnunga,* which embodied material already hundreds of years old. Of that we can be certain due to the section known today as 'The Nine Herbs Charm', for it has references to the pagan gods. Maybe it was not composed in England but came across with Saxon culture from the Continent. Over there, it could already have been hundreds of years old. Even the short extract above echoes the oral tradition that held together Early Saxon culture, with those tantalising glimpses of carts, and bulls and brides. They are all the more fascinating for not being comprehensible, since we have no idea what they were all about !

What is apparent is that in its time they featured significantly in the folk tales and these were so well known that the composer needed only to make brief references in order to bring meaning flooding back into the minds of the listeners. Similarly, from later culture, references to he who robbed the rich to pay the poor remind us of Robin Hood while the highwayman who rode to York reminds us of Dick Turpin's story. These are secular stories, albeit loaded with social justice, whereas the Saxon ones would have derived from the great religious allegories; even our own '*Remember, remember, the fifth of November*' pivots on the conflict between Protestants and Catholics.

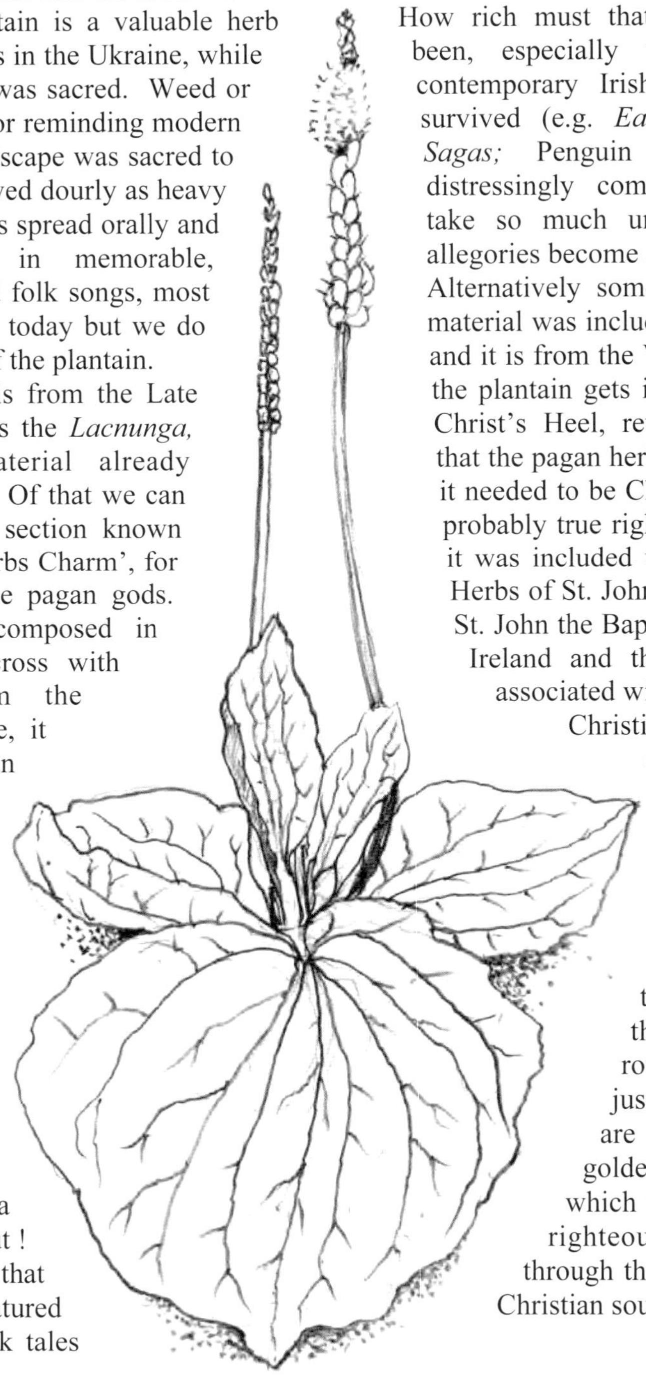

How rich must that Saxon culture have been, especially when we read the contemporary Irish versions that have survived (e.g. *Early Irish Myths and Sagas;* Penguin Classics), rich in distressingly complicated stories, that take so much unravelling before the allegories become apparent. Alternatively some of the early Welsh material was included in the *Mabinogion* and it is from the Welsh *sawdl Crist* that the plantain gets its alternative name of Christ's Heel, revealing straight away that the pagan herb was so powerful that it needed to be Christianised. That was probably true right across Europe since it was included universally among the Herbs of St. John for the celebration of St. John the Baptist at Midsummer. In Ireland and the Isle of Man it is associated with St Patrick.

Christianity was quick to adopt a wide range of wild flowers with which to teach the faith, such as that other little lawn-demon, the daisy. St. Augustine reputedly taught children that they should gather round the one great god just as the daisy petals are gathered around the golden disc in the daisy, which was the golden sun of righteousness shining out through the petals upon all good Christian souls.

PIGS AND THE WINTER SOLSTICE

When the nights were stretching towards their longest it was time to gather for song and story in granddad's hall, to hear of great boar hunts as the time approached for the next. Little boys huddled down between their father's feet to hear of long treks across the pastures, deep into the woods beyond; to hear of the hounds bounding ahead in search of fresh scent over the sodden leaf-fall. The wild boars were elusive. By day they vanished. Somewhere behind barricades of stabbing hawthorn and ripping brambles they slumbered through the light, content to leave their overcoat of long brindled bristles to deal with the incessant dripping of the rain. By night they rooted and hunted and scavenged, with their poor sight discerning only blueness in the lighter parts of darkness. Their simplicity of blue was all the colour vision needed. Hearing was good - a mere mutterance of baying hounds from miles across the valley opened round pigs-eyes. Rising to their feet, boars stood a metre high and two metres long and at a fifth of a tonne they knew how to demolish trouble. Dropping a gape bared tusks in both jaws, with the longest up to 12cm, and with each grinding constantly against the other, the cutting edges were ever sharpened. The baying hounds would dance around on padded feet but keep their distance, just yelling for their masters.[1] The huntsmen lowered their shields to guard their legs and make themselves look wider. Their hands writhed into thrusting position on the spears. They held back. It was time for their catch-dogs, their grippers (think bull terrier types), to lunge in from either side and seize the boar at the base of its ears, away from the tusks. They'd drag the front end of the boar down to the ground and only then did the hunters move in. They gutted it on the spot and tossed the reward to the dogs.

Little boys in the listeners sighed at the success but scars on dog and man had taught respect and caution. Some of their kinsfolk had been killed on boar hunts. Holding a boar at bay required exceptional courage and was not the inevitable ending of a hunt. The boars were far more intelligent and fleet-footed than might be imagined and most got away. To bring one home was a great event. No wonder it became the sport of kings.[2]

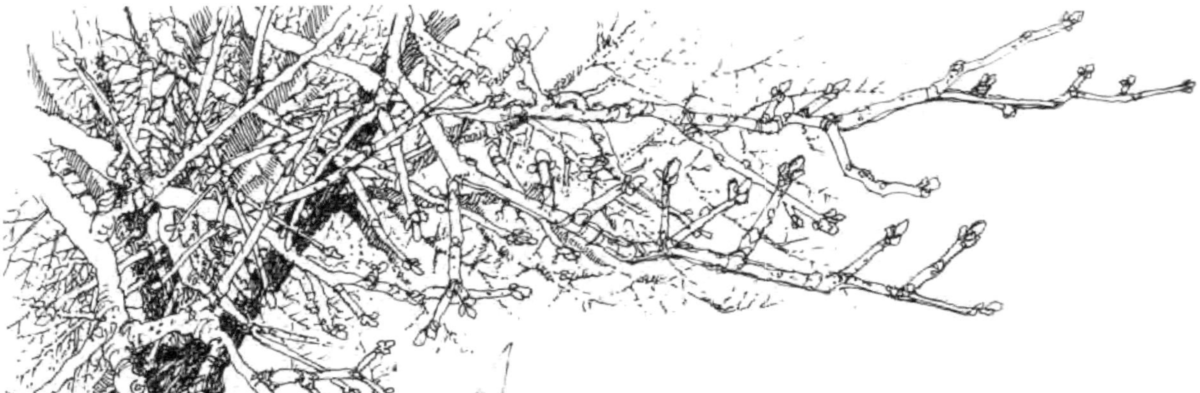

Each telling of the hunt taught the need for this sacrifice each year, ready for the great midwinter rituals at the solstice when the dying sun, growing weaker by the day, would be revived to rise again and warm another season of fertility over the land. They remembered that smell of roast pork drifting through the trees at the temple. They could see again the great boar's head being paraded into their midst, its jaws wedged open with roasted apples: little yellow apples that were symbols of the sun; little apples that were considered the food of the soul and would sustain the soul of the Old Year through the solstice into the New Year. In this way the youngsters were taught the meanings behind the rituals at the temples,[3] were taught the enduring story-lines of the ancient allegories of the faith and would indeed have faith in the great deities of the sun and the sky, the deities of fertility and the deities of war and protection. The wild boar was a totem animal in all categories.

One devout believer was King Rædwald of the East Saxons,[4] for he was the king who converted to Christianity only to have doubts and order the pagan centres to be restored. It is he who was most likely given the famous ship burial at Sutton Hoo, and if Surrey was indeed the 'southern region' of the kingdom of the East Saxons, then we can look upon those grave goods in the British Museum with keener interest. His stunning great helm has become an iconic symbol of Saxon England but look closely at the brazen glowing eyebrows and you will see that they are in fact the bristling backs of a pair of wild boars, looking outwards for approaching danger. Here the boars are totems of protection. More can be seen entwined intricately into the surface decoration of the shoulder clasps. They are not there to intimidate the enemy because enemies were not expected to get close enough to see them. They are there for the all-seeing eyes of the gods of war who would respond with a shield of protection over their adherent. Images of the boar have been found widely in martial contexts and recur in association with the deities of fertility since the boar sired the most offspring.

The wild sows would leave their sounder (family group) a couple of days ahead of farrowing to make a nest in a hollow in the woodland and then give birth in the fresh clean lining of twigs. There could be four, five or six at a time and sometimes even more; she had enough nipples to cater for

twelve. In the nest she would suckle them for the first few days and then take them back to the sounder (protection in numbers; wolves eat piglets) and after a couple of weeks they would be weaned and nosing around excitedly for their own roots and snails and so forth. They changed colour from white, ginger and primrose with umber camouflage patterns to little dark pigs. Throughout this phase the sow was a good mother and remained highly protective. The Saxons were impressed. The boar went off to live a rather solitary life in the woods and became a potent symbol of self-reliance.

At the farmsteads were domesticated versions.[5] These were a bit smaller, at about 70cm, but otherwise looked the same – long body, long snout, thick undercoat of warm dark hair and an overcoat of long blackish bristles to shed the rain. These were particularly lengthy along the spine – long enough for a man to grip and lift the animal, which was a feat of strength for the literary heroes. One difference was the tail. The domesticated pigs had curly tails whereas the wild ones did not. Archaeologists can find skeletal differences (such as the third molar) enabling pig bones to be differentiated between the domesticated and the wild. The latter are now called colloquially 'wild boar' whatever their gender. These differences scotch the old notion that the pigs at home were simply domesticated versions of the wild and that given the chance the two would interbreed. Apparently they were distinct and kept that way.

To see them for real requires a journey far from Surrey, right up to Jarrow, to visit 'Bede's World' (the Museum of Early Medieval Northumbria). There they have back-bred from the European Wild Pig crossed with two old English breeds, the Berkshire and the Tamworth, to get pigs that match as closely as possible the archaeological evidence and later Saxon illustrations.

The Tamworth certainly has the long features of its wild relative but is a surprising bright ginger. The wild pigs have a lot of ginger at first in their paler stripes, so perhaps we should imagine ginger Saxon pigs but any debate over that has been halted by another piece of evidence. The European pig breeds have now been genetically fingerprinted and the Tamworth came up with a particularly singular result; does that mean it is indeed very ancient or does it mean that this breed carries a peculiar combination of genes from later foreign ancestors?[6] Either way, it is a far cry from the round pink cuddlies adored by so many today. Even the name 'pig' is singular. The word does not occur until Late Saxon times and even then is not common. Where the

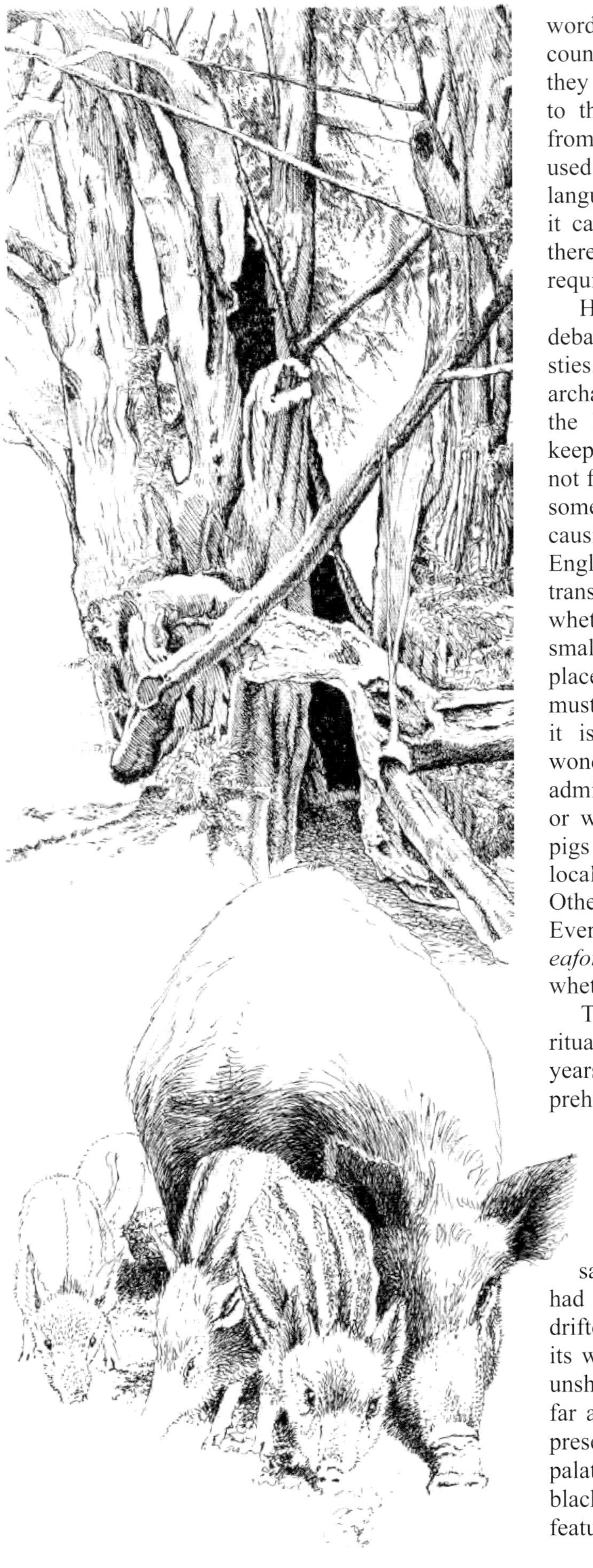

word came from nobody knows. There are counterparts in other Continental languages but they are later and their etymologies trace it back to the English. Where did the English get it from? The same can be asked of 'dog'. Saxons used 'hound' until suddenly there's 'dog' in the language and again nobody knows for sure where it came from, let alone what difference exactly there was between a 'dog' and a 'hound' that required the new word.

How the pigs were kept presents more debate—whether they were free-range or kept in sties. The reply from West Stow was that the archaeologists had looked for post holes around the homes to evidence a wattle surround for keeping toddlers in and pigs out but they could not find that evidence. Bone evidence shows that some pigs at least were tethered by a back leg, causing a deformation of the bone. The Old English language contains *hlose* that gets translated as a pig enclosure or pig shelter but whether that was a large compound or a much smaller sty is not clear. It does give Surrey the place-name Loseley so we know the great estate must go right back to Saxon times. Intriguingly, it is close to Godalming and sets the mind wondering whether this was where the local administration gathered pigs paid in tribute/taxes or whether it perhaps reflects the sacrificing of pigs at the Peper Harow temple site, just as the local Gatwicks could reflect the goat sacrifices. Otherwise attention falls upon the name of Eversheds Farm at Ockley, which derives from *eafor*, the boar, leading Margaret Gelling to query whether it 'might refer to pagan rituals'.[7]

The culling of pigs at the times of the great rituals had been performed for thousands of years. Pig bones are a regular recovery from prehistoric sacred sites. As domestic food they were butchered throughout the year according to need, as evidenced by the recovery of bones from animals of all ages and all seasons. There was no great autumn cull, no mass butchering into joints for salting and smoking up the chimney. They had no chimneys. The smoke from the fires drifted aimlessly round the wooden homes, easing its way out through the thatch, the open door or unshuttered window. It was not concentrated (as far as we know) under a cowl to facilitate meat preservation. The meat might not have been very palatable anyway since it would become coated in black soot very quickly, which is a striking feature when entering the reconstructed home at

West Stow where they fire the hearth and everything gets sooted. A lot of precious salt would be needed too and that might have posed a problem in the early days. Although the Early Saxons did salt meat we do not know whence the main supplies reached Surrey, nor how efficient was the trading service.[8] When Surrey Saxons had pork it was most likely fresh and juicy and, unlike today, the thin layer of fat was of the 'unsaturated' type.

Every part of the pig was used. Yes, it is thought the gut was used for sausage skins and boiled in the cooking pot, and the trotters were boiled in the pot too and soup was made out of tails.[9] The pig was a generous beast. We know nothing about the social viewpoint however, whether a meal of pig trotters was held in low esteem or was a delicacy? There's no indication that they became elitist.

Of some social standing was the job of looking after the pigs. Being the *inswan* (swineherd) was a job of trust and responsibility because he worked for the whole community, paid by them out of the return from the pigs, making it his best interests to ensure they survived and prospered. He came into his own after the corn harvest when the fattening acorns and beech mast were weighty over the woodland trees.[10] His dogs got restless and soon he was gathering up shield and spear and horn and beginning the round-up of the pigs from the community ready to head for the woods and this seasonal bounty of fattening food. It is highly likely this was already an ancient tradition and would of course run out the whole Saxon period. It could not be done today though. For

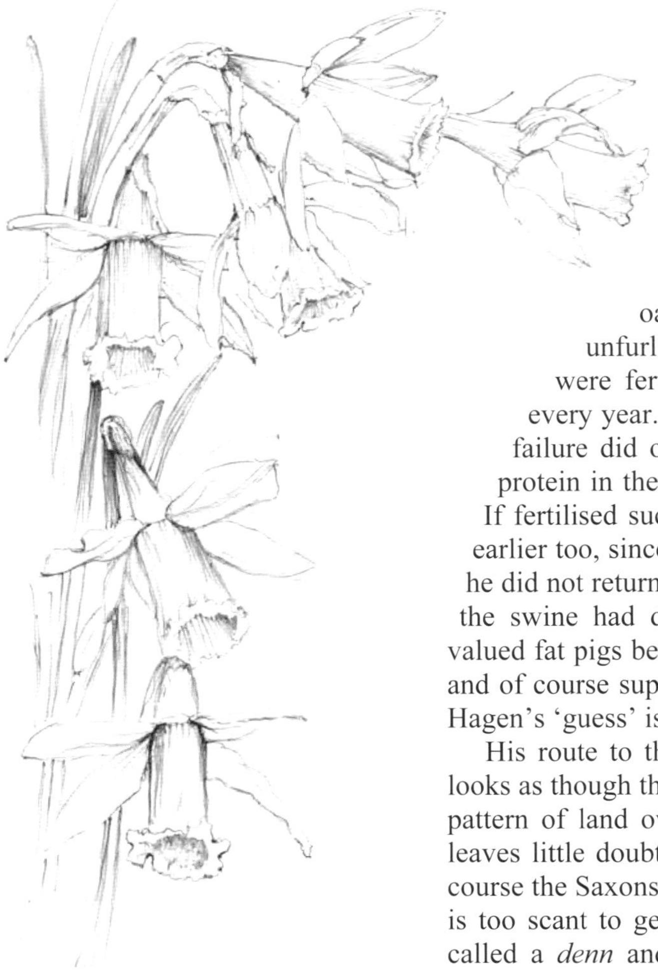

generations it has been noted that there is no such harvest every year. Instead there has been a cycle of high production every three or four years which has become known as the 'mast years'. This implies that the somewhat different winters of Early Saxon times ended earlier, in that there were no late spring frosts when the oaks and beeches burst their catkins out of the unfurling buds. They did not get frost-burnt but were fertilized successfully and developed into mast, every year. Having said that, some people aver that mast failure did occur, leading to chronic shortages of fat and protein in the diet, reflected in the records as famine years. If fertilised successfully it looks as though the mast ripened earlier too, since the *inswan* went off at the end of August and he did not return until the beginning of the New Year. By then the swine had doubled or even trebled their weight. They valued fat pigs because the high calorie count gave them energy and of course supplied the essential fat component in their diet. Hagen's 'guess' is that 10-15% of a carcass was fat.[11]

His route to the woods was along ancient trackways, for it looks as though the Saxons used a pre-existing system within the pattern of land ownership and usage. It is so intricate that it leaves little doubt that it had been long in the making. In due course the Saxons expanded upon this but in Surrey the evidence is too scant to get a clear picture. A swine pasture was often called a *denn* and so across the Wealden forest area of Kent there are plenty of place-names ending in 'den' to indicate where this transhumance was happening. In Wealden Sussex there are far fewer while in Surrey there are precious few.[12] Maybe this says more about the language of the differing peoples than about their agriculture. Maybe the element *–falod* should be included, if it means a 'fold' for livestock, as at Chiddingfold, Dunsfold, Alfold and with more over the Sussex border. There's no indication that it has to mean a sheep fold but could enclose any livestock.[13] Indeed it is difficult to imagine these borderlands in the Wealden forest being prime sheep country. Then there are the places ending in –ber deriving from *bearu* for a small wood and which could well have been swine pastures.[14] All in all, the evidence led John Blair to assert "it is unquestionable that numerous Wealden settlements in Surrey began as swine-pastures."[15] The Saxons in England made the pig more common than did the Germanic people on the Continent.

Some of the swine-pastures were a long trudge from home (swine from Sutton had their *denn* near Horley[16] which was about fifteen miles on the map but much more by meandering trackway). If the pigs came from smallish sties they presumably took great delight in their freedom, before settling down to the expedition, and so extra members of the community may well have joined in with the herding until the swine tired and settled down. It has been said (without citing evidence) that they were relatively easy to control, which would be a far cry from so many of today's stied pigs whose one delight pivots upon bolting for freedom, to burst their way through any gap of light (there's so much truth in saying a bow-legged man wouldn't stop a pig in a passage). The *inswan* had to stop them all wandering off and that might have given him a problem with the dimming of light intensity after the autumn equinox for this triggered their sexual activity, and then after mating[17] they would want to wander off on their own away from the sounder. He probably had one boar for every dozen sows, judging by the Welsh laws, so having even four or five of those could well have tried his patience.[18]

Being in the woods was worth the effort. What a feast they had and not just of mast, for the swineherd would have beaten down all manner of fruits from overhead branches, such as crab apples, checkers and sloes. They in turn plundered deep into the woodland floor with their snouts for anything else that might be there, such as bulbs, tubers, rhizomes etc. They divested the ground of the lot so that after a few years the swine-pastures would be recognisable for being so bare and brown. Springtime did not roll out its colourful carpets of bluebells or golden daffodils[19] after *Efniht* (even night; the spring equinox). These were the glories of the coppices, where it would have made sense for the destructive swine to have been banned. The ground flora of the coppices was one that had adapted, since at least the Iron Age, to the cycles of light and shade between the cropping of the tree stools. During the shade years they survived on their own food stores – bulbs for the bluebells (*illus. right*) and daffodils (*illus. left*), starchy rhizomes for wood anemones and bracken, bulbils for wood sorrel, tubers for lesser celandines, fleshy crowns for primroses, they all had their expedient and the swine had gone home before they bloomed and gave away their locations. Any in the swine-pastures would have been devoured although they had self protection expedients too, such as the caustic sap in wood anemones, lesser celandines and wood sorrel. The starchy crowns of the male fern are enjoyed by livestock but would have caused thiamine deficiency disease. Did the *inswan* know that? Whether bracken rhizomes were already carcinogenic at that time is not known but they

remained pig food till the 1940s.[20] All in all, imagine the swine-pasture woodlands as brown desolations, pitted with flooded wallow holes. Today's pigs won't wallow but Saxon ones loved it. The mud and water kept them cool and probably cleansed them of parasites and other cohabitants in their coats.[2] They must have loved their annual sojourn in the woods.

The *inswan* may have found it a bit lonesome, although he may have taken his family with him. They had a temporary *sumerhus* (summerhouse) and this appears in a very late document cited by Blair, "the yearly 'sumerhus' which Shellwood tenants were still obliged to build in 1226 had originally been for the lord's use when he came to inspect the pannage in late summer."[22] Did such visits provide welcome company or did they constitute that grand English condemnation of 'poking their nose in'? Did the *inswan* moan because he was expected to shave before presenting himself? It is easy to think that he didn't bother to shave while he was out there but it is just as likely that he did, out of respect to his gods. Surely he did on 'Fridays' when he honoured Friga, goddess of fertility,[23] along with her brother Frea/Frey. These great fertility deities could quite possibly have been different aspects of the overall concept of the Great Earth Mother,[24] thought to have been Nerthus.

The deities of the boar were all important to him; they gave him fortitude in the wilderness. It was to them he had made his vows for the coming year at the sacrifice of the boar at the winter solstice and to remind him of those vows he may well have worn a boar-tusk talisman round his neck, that would go with him to the grave. For the moment we can picture him at the edge of the wood enjoying the last warmth of the sun in *winterfilleth* (winterfilled; October) as he looks out over the adjoining pasture. Seasonal flocks of birds had arrived from the north to probe amid the tussocks making little grey hunchbacks among the grasses. These fieldfares he called *fealu fearh* or 'grey piglet'. (illus. opp.)

END NOTES

1 These are 'bay' dogs because of their baying and kept the boar 'at bay' until hunters arrived. The grippers are 'catch' dogs such as today's Pit Bull Terrier and Staffordshire Bull Terrier.

2 It was also vital 'pest control' in the early days when boars were commoner because a single boar could devastate a small Saxon field of barley in a single night.

3 Saxon religion followed an oral tradition and was never written down. The little we know about it has to be pieced together from incidental references.

4 Died c.625.

5 European Wild Pig is classified as Sus scrofa whereas the smaller domestic version is Sus scrofa pallustris and originated probably by cross breeding with a wild pig from South East Europe; Weissman 86.

6 www.tamworthbreedersclub.co.uk/10.html.

7 Gelling p.175.

8 Supplies possibly from Essex, which was one of the main production areas; Pryor 2004.

9 Hagen (1995) p.111.

10 "A single well grown Oak tree would serve to produce well over 100lbs of pork per year." Hagen (1995) p.106.

11 Hagen (1995) p.121.

12 Blair p.51.

13 Blair p.51.

14 See Hagen (1995) p.110 plus Gelling (2003) pp.221-3.

15 Blair p.51.

16 Blair p.19.

17 Mating was normally Oct/Nov and gestation took about 115 days, so farrowing occurred with the uprising of spring growth when extra feed was most needed.

18 Male piglets not destined for breeding were castrated and became known as a barg/bearg, which had equivalents in the other Germanic languages, and gives us the modern current term 'barrow'.

19 Snowdrops were yet to be introduced, in the later Middle Ages.

20 By then we butchered pigs at too early an age for carcinomas to be apparent.

21 Being dark-skinned, they didn't get sunburn like today's pink pigs.

22 Blair p.55.

23 Fertility should be understood broadly to encompass goddess of love and lust, of marriage and all aspects of midwifery and childbirth, as well as the fertility of the soil to produce crops. Some people think the faith persists in the notion of the 'Harvest Queen'. Friga was the wife of Wodan and believed by some to have given her name to the place-names of Freefolk, Froyle and Frobury over the Hampshire border.

24 Their faith was primarily matriarchal. Tacitus, writing back in the 1st century, reported that the Suebic tribes in the north and east of the Elbe basin worshipped the Mother of the Gods. Her sacred animal was the boar and Tacitus says the tribes (such as the Aestii from the Prussian coast) adopted it to ensure her protection, saying they bore the shape of the animal, which is taken to refer to boar masks in the rites, precursors of the boar banners carried ahead of later warriors. The hero of Beowulf did just that and had a wondrous boar's-head helmet. Plutarch reported such helmets being worn by the Cimbri tribe. Archaeologists have recovered several of them so the imagery in Beowulf derives from truth and is not literary invention. Such finds came from Sutton Hoo, Suffolk; Benty Grange, Derbyshire; Wollaston, Northamptonshire, and Coppergate, York.

The powerful image remained current long after conversion to Christianity and was used by Cynewulf in his poem Elene, wherein Constantine was sleeping under the sign of the boar at the time of his vision of the Cross, so it bridges the gap between the two religions.

ILLUSTRATIONS

Wild Pig illustrations from sketches made originally in France (1970s) and at the former Norfolk Wildlife Centre, now The Animal Ark (1980s). The women pig-shifters are shown with besoms because that is what we used in my childhood and the word 'besom' is Saxon so we know they had them. They also had the word 'broom' but we do not know what differences there were between their perceptions of the two tools.

HAY, HORSES AND WET WEATHER

Ah, hay-making! Doesn't that somehow chime of long, hot, sunny summers back in a Golden Age when Englishmen worked the land in harmony with Mother Nature? Huh! It was an exhausting, back-breaking race between the thunder clouds that sweet Mother Nature so inexcusably sent at the wrong time. Was this known to our Early Saxons?

It is said by some that hay-making was a Saxon invention and not an introduction by the Romans, who had sailed out of warmer winters where they had no need of it. Hay, it is argued, was horse feed and the Romans in Britain were not horse-orientated but marched everywhere. That argument implies there were very few horses here. In fact the British had been breeding them since before the Romans even came and some breeds survive, like the Dartmoor and the Exmoor. Apart from that, horses were not the *only* livestock to need winter feed supplements.

The notion of there being no hay in Iron Age and Roman Britain stirred doubt and disbelief. Could it really have been an Early Saxon invention? The language does not support that. The word 'hay' was given to us by the Saxons, as their Old English *heg, hig* or *hieg*. In Old Frisian it was *ha* or *he*. In Old Saxon it was *hoi*. In Old High German it was *hewi* or *houwi*. In Old Norse it was *hey*. If hay was such a late invention how did all these different cultures end up coining basically the same word for it? Furthermore, the same can be said for the tool used for cutting it, the scythe, for that too occurs across the languages of North West Europe. The hay-making verb 'to ted' has equivalents in Old Norse and Old High German. When the people who spoke these languages sailed up the Thames they knew already about hay.

Furthermore, when they explored the countryside they would have seen the Romano-British tedding, because the Romans did practise it. It was in their best interests to share their knowledge with the natives in order to increase production and there were at least eleven, and probably fifteen, Romanised estates in Surrey.[1] Their well-read visitors could have viewed the meadows and commented upon the readiness for mowing, in accordance with top Roman writers such as Cato, Columella, Palladius, Pliny and Varro :-

"*Cut hay when it is ready, and take care not to be too late in cutting. Cut before the seed is ready, and put up the best hay by itself.*" Cato. cap III

"*Hay should be cut before it begins to wither, for, in this situation, it produces a larger crop, and affords pleasanter food for cattle.*" Columella. Lib. I. cap XLIX

"*In May, in dry, warm, or maritime places, hay may be cut, but before it withers.*" Palladius. Lib. VI. tit.I.

"*The time of cutting is when the stalk begins to lose the flowers and to harden: It ought to be cut before it withers.*" Pliny. Nat. Hist. Lib. XVIII. cap XXVIII

"*Whenever grass ceases to grow, and begins to wither with the heat, it ought to be cut with scythes.*" Varro. Lib. I cap XLIX

All this was sound advice, designed to catch the flowers and grasses at their richest in sugars and nitrogen compounds, as they turned from flower to seed. Catching that moment was crucial, before it scorched in the hot Mediterranean sun, but in Britain the season moved a little slower. Thus to mow in May, as per Palladius, was too early. Instead, they watched for the flowering of the beautiful pink Ragged Robin,[2] which came a fraction later than the choice hay plants, signalling that they would be on the turn. That was not in May but in June, when the pagans celebrated Midsummer. This got Christianised as St. Barnabas Day.[3]

Put your scythe to the grass
Upon St. Barnabas Day.

The equal hours of day and night are reflected in the lore

When Barnabas smiles both night and day
Poor Ragged Robin blooms in the hay.

Even June was often too early in Britain but the Church was disseminating lore from Rome. At various periods in Surrey history, such as the mid 19th century, it was normal to cut hay on the uplands in June; thus George Sturt (writing as George Bourne) recorded that:

Given a cloak against the wet; any type of head gear is conjectural because evidence has not survived.

Ragged Robins

"With June comes in the airy upland hay-making; that of the deep water-meadows follows it close."[4]

Similarly, back in 1635 Gervase Markham advised that he "*would have every good husbandman, about a week after Midsummer, to view his meadows well. And if he sees them turn brown, if the cocks heads of the grass turn downwards and stand not upright; if the bells and other vessels of seed stand open and shed their seeds; if your honeysuckles [clovers] have lost their flowers, and the pennygrass be dry, hard and withered; then shall you well and truly understand that your meadow is ripe and ready to be mown.*" (The English Gentleman)

July is the favoured month nowadays and so it was by the end of the Saxon period for that is the month where the meticulous line of a Saxon illustrator showed it on the Julius Work Calendar of about 1020. He drew three scythesmen busy mowing while a fourth sharpened his scythe. A fifth wielded a spade and was perhaps digging out noxious perennials like Ragwort. The sixth labourer he leant on his scythe watching (there's always one!). This tiny masterpiece is believed to have been produced in the scriptorium of Canterbury Cathedral and so is likely to reflect the English agricultural year rather than the Mediterranean.

Our imaginings should have the Saxons mowing in June only in good warm years. Even that was probably too late to be accompanied by the last stuttering call of the cuckoo.[5] More likely the cuckoo had migrated south already, just echoing in the memory and through the imagery of the Saxon poetry. Perchance it was the Saxons who first observed that

The first cock of hay
Frightens the cuckoo away.

Cocks of hay across the July fields must have been so heartening. They meant the cutting and tedding had been completed, leaving only the garnering into outdoor ricks or under a rainproof roof. It was a crop of major importance, since the future for man and beast depended upon getting through the next winter, so they took a lot of trouble over it. This must

Cuckoo

have made mowing a particularly prolonged and arduous task on the Romanised estates if they were doing it according to 'the book'. Roman writers decreed that mowers should not cut the meadows just once but should go over them again a second time. Pliny told them "as meadows are cut, the mowers must come over them again, and cut what they leave the first time," because the grasses would bolt up to seed and "*it is improper to allow the plants to rise to the seed, which the grass passed over by the mowers will certainly do....*"[6] Cutting the whole lot short would have ensured a good return of 'bottom growth' from the crowns as fodder or for an autumn mowing. It would also have retarded species like cocksfoot from forming tussocks that would impede the scythe in the future.

Similarly, Varro informed them "*the meadow must be mowed again, that is, the grass cut, which the mowers pass by, who leave the field ridged by the grass.*"[7]

Ridges would also make mowing the more difficult in the future and leaving material behind was wasting some of the current harvest. Roman texts certainly instructed how to get the best out of the land and therefore the Romanised estates in Surrey could well have set high standards. We do not know to what extent those standards were perpetuated or for how long. That said, since the number of livestock owned became a crucial social factor it would be logical to imagine Saxons doing their utmost to get as many beasts through the lean time of the year as possible and to that end would have mowed thoroughly.

It would be very interesting to know whether they mowed again, as a regular practice, in September, as advocated in the Roman texts, where this second harvest was accorded the name *cordum*. It is made to sound very desirable by Columella who observed "*for this is softer, and, on that account, sweeter than the hay come to its full growth.*"[8] A warm dry autumn after a good summer's growth would surely have prompted the Saxons to mow again – oh dear, more backache! Skeletal defects due to hard labour have been attributed to staggering around with part-bent knees under heavy loads and this would have been exacerbated by the sweeping action of scything. Obviously the full effects cannot be appreciated without knowing how much meadow a Saxon would have mown and there is no way of answering that. We can be sure that the work was intensive because it had to be achieved in the short phases of good weather, with the constant fear that storms might over-ride them. This was not a job that could be done little by little each day until completed comfortably. The Roman writers expected their mowers to scythe an *iugerum* per day[9] (about five eighths of an acre), which sounds reasonable but in reality would have tested their endurance. Their muscles were not used to the swinging motion of scything. There were just a few back-straightening breaks for sharpening the scythe on a whetstone. It was best to wipe the blade first to prevent the green sap on it from clogging the texture of the stone but that depended in part on the type of stone employed. Maybe the Saxons did not bother, depending upon the ease with which they could replace a clogged whetstone.

Attention always focuses upon the mower but it was a team effort. Some credit must be given to the equally relentless labouring of the team following the scythe. They had to hook out the swathes to wilt, with a hayfork, which they had cut from a forked growth in the hedgerow. It required a good degree of dexterity, to flick out the grass into an even distribution over the land and again there was a lot of that painful swinging motion. If the job went to a woman it was certainly not an easy option, even if they did have strong wrists. It was relentless, with just brief interruptions to pick out stems of deadly ragwort and savage thistles or upon flicking out a *snaka* (grass snake). The snake was a revered beast whose part in their allegories was of ancient standing. How odd that the Christians should cast it as evil and make people fearful.

Once the tedded grass had wilted and dried the bundling could begin. Again we get an insight from the same Roman writers, who expected a good worker to bind 1200 bundles a day. That does sound a lot. Even with the long English summer giving some sixteen hours between sunrise and sunset (ignoring the possibility of continuing by the light of the moon), it still meant tying a bundle every 48 seconds non stop. It does not actually take that long, once the binder has got the knack of pulling out some long grasses, twisting them into a bond and securing it round – but to keep that up for hour after hour is a different matter. The Romans expected each bundle to weigh four of their pounds. If we convert that into a daily total measured in the more familiar avoirdupois it means the binder shifted 1.6 tons of hay!

Of course that is only what the writers decreed; it was an ideal rather than a measurement of regular achievement. Nevertheless, payment was probably calculated on that basis and so it would have been a working target. Probably some of the Roman estates in Surrey tried to maintain that into the 5th century while independent farmers on neighbouring lands felt less pressured. Nevertheless, dark rain clouds mounting the western skies would harry the workers as relentlessly as any Roman bailiff. That hay harvest was too precious to lose.

Across the meadow we need to imagine the mowers with their scythes and behind them the tedders with their hayforks. Those would be followed, after wilting and drying, by rakers, who presumably raked the hay into lots of about 4lb each, ready for the binders. They would have bound and moved on, leaving the bundles for somebody else to group together in pyramidal stooks or cocks,[10] to get them up in the air to continue drying. If the sky gods were unimpressed and sent rain then the haymakers tried to dry it better by draping it over wigwams of poles with a few horizontal wattles woven round to support the bundles.[11]

Once thoroughly dried, the stooks were combined into one big *hreac* (rick). That's when they discovered that if stacked too damp it all heated up and taught them a lesson in spontaneous combustion! That was a disaster since that safeguard against the lean months could not be replaced. The only insurance policy was faith in the gods. People had been seeking portents of favour from those gods for over five months:

A warm February
A bad hay crop.

If in February there be no rain
Twill bring no hay or grain.

When April blows his horn
Tis good for hay and corn.

Flowers in May
Good cocks of hay.

A wet May
Brings a big load of hay.

We do not know the age of these observations but doubtless Early Saxons construed their own versions. Their whole existence depended upon the success of the harvest and so weather lore was not going to get superseded by assurances of everlasting life from the expanding Christian Church, which therefore had to embrace it:-

Rain on Good Friday and Easter Day,
A good year for grass; a bad year for hay.

A wet Good Friday and Saturday
Brings plenty of grass but little hay.

If it rains on Easter Day
Be good for grass but bad for hay.

A good deal of rain on Easter Day
Gives good crop of corn but little good hay.

Cocksfoot
Sheep's Fescue
Sweet Vernal
False Oat

Theoretically the Church would have preferred to abolish weather lore (despite its presence in the Bible) because it implied predestination which was not part of its doctrine. That was a pagan concern whereby fertility rituals were performed in supplication for a good harvest and then they looked for signs as to whether their wishes would be granted. Is there an echo of those pagan times in the Church ritual of taking Ragged Robin, together with Sweet Woodruff and Dog Roses, for making into Barnaby Garlands to invoke the saint as a peacemaker – very useful with the fury of a thunderstorm bearing down upon the meadows, but is it truly Christian?

How interesting it would be to know how the pagan versions ran. The eye-catching reddening of the skies doubtless betokened actions of the sky gods – red streaks to the Vikings were trailing strands of Thor's great red beard as he hurtled by in another of his impulsive outrages. Similar tantrums would have been attributed to his Saxon counterpart, Thunor (hence 'thunder'). When the heavens broke "it rained cats and dogs," which is thought by some to derive from the totem animals of the pagan sky/weather deities. All cultures attributed the weather to the power of the gods, so as the Saxons became Christian they encountered Judaic lore:

> "*Fair weather cometh out of the north: with God is terrible majesty.*"
> (Job 37.22).

Therein they also encountered the ever popular

Red sky at night, shepherds' delight.
Red sky at morning, shepherds' warning.

which occurs in Matthew's Gospel (16:2-3), "*When it is evening, ye say, It will be fair weather: for the sky is red. And in the morning, It will be foul weather to day: for the sky is red and louring.*" (Authorised Version; pub. 1611).[12]

Red was always the colour of the gods and it is an odd colour that will not sit comfortably amid others. A red object is difficult to place in its true perspective and so soon became the colour of

military attire, to confuse the enemy. The Roman army in Britain used it and had a trade in the red dye, made from madder roots,[13] but when the legions left they took that trade with them. The remaining peoples preferred yellow, blue and green and all the natural tones in the sheep fleeces, even though British plants would have provided a much wider range with some beautiful colours. Perhaps life on the farms was too busy for much fussing over dyes; they tended to restrict the more precious colours to borders of tablet weave on their costumes, and for their belts and bags.[14] As the period progressed so the use of red dye increased along with their wealth and power, until it was soon signifying high status and royalty. To hold that required men-at-arms and they too donned red tunics, as a military tactic and a social signal.[15]

Surrey was completely hemmed in by warring neighbours: East Saxons, Jutes, South Saxons, West Saxons and Mercian Angles. From pioneer beginnings arose powerful royal realms, numbering ten at their peak, until conquest reduced these into one, in 829.[16] Many times the red-clad warriors must have bled across Surrey in their hundreds, reputations enfolded in their special tunics, legs flailing without stirrups, honour behind their shields, victory pointing their spears. Victory would be theirs, for had they not called upon Wodan to ride at their sides? Had they not called up their ancestral spirits through the sacred ash tree that shafted their spears? They fought at *Wibandun*,[17] they fought at *Aclea*,[18] they fought wherever needed, to be 'King of all England'.

Hundreds of horsemen trotted off to battle because that was how they got there. Then they dismounted and fought on foot, with their horses watching from the sidelines. They were still small horses, very similar to Exmoor ponies, although the notion of 'pony' had yet to be invented. Do not under-estimate them though, for even if only three feet high at the shoulder they could carry a 12 stone warrior for 40 miles.[19] Even so, to these ancient breeds the Romans had introduced fresh bloodstock, largely from the Scythian horse, which was larger and faster, and thereby increased the variety in England - so varied that the archaeologists at Newstead found six different types of which one was reckoned to have been as good as today's Arab horses.[20]

There seems to have been a wide colour range too, with the royal warriors in *Beowulf* riding chestnuts. Perhaps that had become the elitist colour although later English documents record royal gifts of horses in all colours. There would have been piebalds and skewbalds in the landscape because the ancient breeds included white ones. Let us not argue whether

they were in fact 'greys' with black skin under the white hair, or true 'whites' with pink skin, because I have no idea what colour skin was under the hair of a Saxon horse. What we do know is that white horses were of ancient origin, sacred to the prehistoric peoples, with their sanctity coming through to the Early Saxons, causing the Christian Church to ban the eating of horse meat due to its intense pagan associations. Greatest of these horse cults was that of Epona, the great white mare, traceable right across Europe and therefore well known to the founders of the Early Christian Church. It made the animal a powerful totem, reflected in the choice of personal names like Hengist and Horsa, both of which meant the horse, derived from *hors* meaning swiftness. Two brothers, sons of Wihgils, bearing those same names, resound through the stories of the supposed 'migration' period. We read that they were brought over as mercenaries by Vortigern in his fight to keep Britain free from Rome but their success inspired rebellion against him and opened the country to settlement by the Germanic peoples. Thus in the Anglo-Saxon Chronicle for 455 it records,..

"*In this year Hengist and Horsa fought against King Vortigern at a place called Aegelesthrep [Aylesford, Kent] and Horsa was slain. After that Hengist succeeded to the kingdom.*"

And in 456

"*In this year Hengist and his son, Aesc fought against the Britons at a place called Crecganford: [Crayford, Kent] and there slew four companies and the Britons then forsook Kent and fled to London in great terror.*"

The dates may not be entirely accurate but there are those who say the whole story is invention, nothing more than a later creation myth to explain the origins of the new nation. That seems a bit extreme since a written creation myth needed to embody nuggets of truth reflecting the known 'truths' held in oral tradition.[21]

What an oral tradition it must have been too, for the people loved story-telling and bequeathed us such masterpieces as *Beowulf* and *The Battle of Maldon*. Through these writings we too can ride with the *horshere* (mounted force) along the *horsweg* (bridle-way) and care for our overlord's mounts as his *horswealh* (groom) before turning them out for the night into the *horsgærstun* (horse meadow). The need for horse caring (*horsweard*) gave rise to occupation and social rank alike, just as it gave prominence to centres of excellence for good brood mares, such as Horsham out in the Wealden grasslands of Sussex. In Surrey, the Horsley's are believed to take their name from the clearing of downland woods to make horse pastures.[22] Horsleydown is less easy to imagine, being now swamped by Brixton, but reminding us that 'south London' places were service areas for the increasingly important Saxon settlement at Southwark on the Surrey bank of the Thames. Horsemen were continually on the move through there, needing hay for their mounts, just as the milk-and-meat livestock needed hay too. The Saxons did not invent hay – they prayed to their sky-gods for the fine weather to make it.

END NOTES

1 Map of them, p.9, The Roman Temple at Wanborough booklet from the Surrey Archaeological Soc.

2 Ragged Robin may have been called butul but another suggestion has it as the name for Cuckoo Flower, Cardamine pratensis.

3 Changed from 24th June of the old Julian calendar to 11th June when England adopted the Gregorian Calendar in 1752.

4 *Lucy Bettesworth*; p.20. Although published in 1913 it was a compilation of recollections of the mid 19th century when Lucy was young. What Sturt committed to print normally proves to be accurate.

5 Cuckoo is the name introduced by the Normans that replaced the Old English geac, which survives in some dialect names such as gowke in the north of England; Lockwood 49-50. It occurs in place-names too, e.g. Yagdon, Shropshire; Gelling and Cole 169.

6 Pliny; Nat. Hist. Lib. XVIII. Cap. XXVIII.

7 Varro. Lib. I. cap. XLI.

8 Col. Lib. VII cap.II.

9 "A good mower cuts an iugerum of meadow…" Columella. Lib. XI. Cap.II; "It is one day's work of a man, to mow a iuerum…" Pliny; Nat. Hist.; Lib. XVIII. Cap. XXVIII.

10 Both terms are likely to have come from the Norse and to have had Saxon equivalents,e.g. there is evidence that there was an Old English word cocc now lost to us but preserved in place-names.

11 Still remembered being practised in Surrey in mid 20th century.

12 The Wyclif Bible of 1395 read, "The eeuenynge maad, ye seien, It shal be cleer, for the heuene is lijk to reed; and the morwe, To day tempest, for heuen shyneth heuy, or sorwful."

13 Best madder was from the dried roots of Rubia tinctoria, imported probably from France. The native Rubia peregrina gave an inferior colour and probably did not grow in Surrey. Here they

could have used a related plant, lady's bedstraw, Gallium verum, but again the colour was inferior. See Rogers.

14 Rogers, p.63, lists a few examples from excavations.

15 It should not be presumed that all warriors wore red at all times. It probably began as a run-on from the Roman military presence and gathered momentum as new power bases emerged into the Early Saxon kingdoms. It is probably safe to presume it was worn whenever the wearer was on 'official business'.

16 King Egbert of Wessex (r.802-839) was the first to be known as king of all England, in 829, but that did not include Northern England. He became overlord of Wales in 831.

17 Battle of Wibandun, 568, between Ceawlin of Wessex and Æthelbert of Kent for supremacy over Surrey. Site often reckoned to be at Wimbledon but there are strong aguments for Windlesham. See Malden, and Stevens.

18 Battle of Aclea, between Æthelwulf and the Danes, 851 acc. To Anglo-Saxon Chron. May have been in Surrey at Ockley.

19 Urquart, p.119.

20 Urquart, p.118.

21 For an objective summary of sources and modern opinion upon Hengist and Horsa etc. see Henson. Also for the literature refs.

22 But not Horsell, which according to Gover p.128 derives from horig, meaning foul or dirty, so the place-name would be muddy shelf or slope, and the peaty boggy terrain behind the present residential suburb would fit this.

Horsetails (Equisetum spp.) are cursed by gardeners today and likewise the mowers of yesteryear. Pliny informing the Romans about hay-field plants said, "the best is trefoil, the next is common grass, the worst is the mimmulus: the hard siliqua likewise, and the plant called equisetis, on account of its resemblance to a horse's tail, are hated by the mower" (Pliny. Nat. Hist. Lib. XVIII. Cap XXV111).

This was because it blunted the scythes from having the richest source of silica (sand) crystals. This made it very useful for scowering pots and polishing wood and metal (including their jewellery) but ruined the sharp edge on a scythe.

***

Ragwort (lower) was probably called 'boden' and the Saxons must have been aware that it was dangerous. It contains pyrrolizidine alkaloids, which are not toxic until they are digested and then they are converted into dangerous metabolites. These are stored in the body until a lethal level is reached but a large intake can produce rapid results so the Saxons would have been able to associate cause and effect. Drying it in hay concentrates the poison and also renders it more palatable. They would have picked it out.

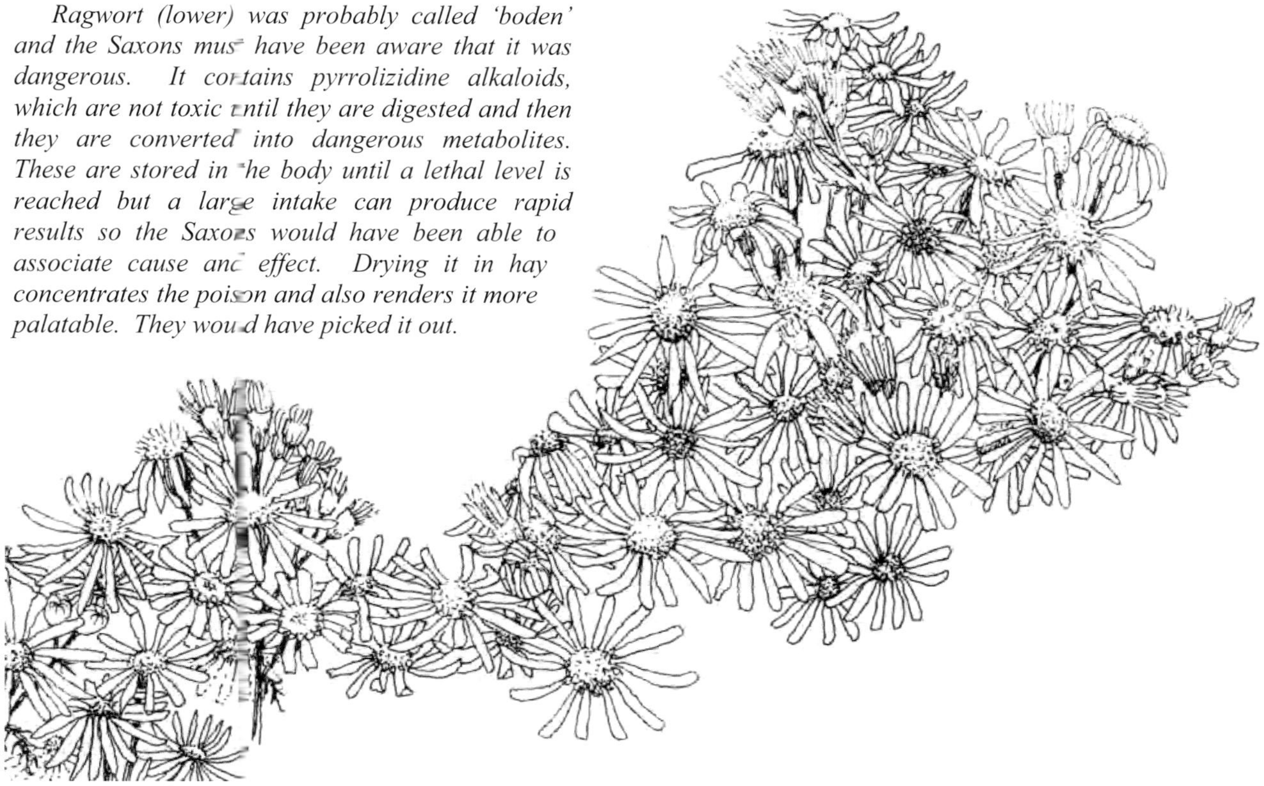

CEREALS, BREAD AND THE HARVEST

Thin sunlight filtered through the spring mist to slant through the framing of the open-sided building at West Stow as I changed places with the archaeologist to try my hand at milling corn with the hand quern. It was a rotary quern, with a big bottom stone overtopped with another, which gave me the idea it was going to take some shifting. How wrong I was. That top stone trundled round and round as easily as could be, since the grain I trickled into the top acted like ball bearings. They were racing out the sides like ball bearings too. The stones had only chipped them but I was told to scoop them up and filter them back in. Gradually there were fewer and fewer ball bearings and more and more flour. It took only about twenty minutes to grind enough flour for a loaf I was told, prompting me to exclaim that the books were quoting far greater time spans for the job. That, I was told, was because some archaeologists have made the mistake of testing excavated examples, which had become worn out and thrown away by the Saxons. With a freshly cut stone, such as I was using, the task was quick and easy. How right she was. Flour was piling round the quern in a very satisfying manner. If I was aiming for flour evenly graded I would need to sieve it through a cloth as the Saxons did but for a rough-and-ready belly-filler this would have been fine.

The bread oven nearby looked massive and would take a lot of really big loaves. Wrong – big ovens were for small loves and big loaves went into small ovens I was told. The big ovens would charge so hot that they would crust the outside of a big loaf before the middle was cooked, so only small loaves were put in there. It was the small oven that released a more moderate heat to bake a big loaf right through.

It seemed all very logical and simple as the top stone trundled round and round in that pool of sunlight. Of course there were days when the winter easterlies off the North Sea would have driven iced rain-arrows through instead. Whatever the weather, this was a daily task and any change in the rumbling of the stones would have alerted the head of the house that her children or slaves were beginning to slacken. We might smile sympathetically at that thought but only because our notion of food has changed. To the Early Saxons bread was central to their whole sense of wellbeing. Their notion of a meal was bread. It provided them with their carbohydrate and B-group vitamins. Anything else, be it meat or fish, eggs or cheese, fruit or vegetables, was simply an extra, for flavouring, variety and health. Thus the weather was all important since none of their other produce relied to the same extent upon the right weather at the right time. They wanted dry spells for ploughing and harrowing, wind-free days for sowing and then warm rain for germination followed by sun and showers to grow the corn on, before really warm dry weather for ripening and harvesting. Then it could rain again, to soften the ground for ploughing once more. They searched the natural world for portends of what was to come. For interpretations they would have turned to the men who grew the corn, for surely nobody studied it more closely, with the possible exception of the priests.

All watched for the waxing of the moon before sowing so that the growing larger of the moon would draw growth out of the seeds.[1] Then, of course, they made the right observances to the deity of the moon on the *Monan daeg* (Moon's day, Monday)

Fortunately the weather in the South East gets less rain than the west and plenty of sunshine. There would have been good conditions for corn and that must have made up much of the cropping in the Thames Valley portion of Surrey. The ploughmen were glad it was flat and the soils of river alluvium were fairly fertile. The land was

less fertile where the soil was sand and pebbles outwashed from the Ice Age glaciers but at least there were no rocks. The Downland farmers had their ards striking impediments of flint while the heathland farmers contended with big purple shards of ironstone, so the Thames Valley was one of the easiest places to use the ard. It was not followed by women and slaves picking stones and heaving off basketfuls of them. Instead, this was where they worried about summer floods, where the Wey, Mole and Bourne all lost their pace in a congestion of reed beds.

Winter floods were a worry too because the farmers practised autumn sowing as well as spring. Seed was sown broadcast, by flinging handfuls to either side while walking across the fields. I remember doing it just once when I was a child, perhaps filling in a swathe that had not germinated well. What I do remember is how my arm ached! You needed a really wide swing to get a good even spread and save yourself from the bare brown ridicules of uneven germination. To keep on a true line meant crossing the land between two markers, keeping eyes fixed on the one ahead. That was moved up two paces upon reaching it, before returning to the other. Can't you just imagine the Saxons doing that – knifing a marker stake out of the hedge and lancing the bark off the top so that the white wood could be seen right across the field?

This task doesn't suit wind, so imagine the Saxons doing it on a calm day, with enough sun to warm the soil for rapid germination, even though the season was calling out the woollen cloaks, with the fading of the summer. Along the field edge, imagine sun-goldened hawthorns, heavy with trusses of their deep red agasses (haws).[2] It is too early for them to be stripped by the *thrisce* (thrush) and the redwings (*illus. opp.*). Bones of both these birds have been unearthed in the food waste at *Hamwic* (Southampton), bearing knife marks from where the meat had been cut off. Although this evidence is from the mid-Saxon period there is no reason to conclude earlier Saxons didn't hunt along the hedgerows when the autumn migration flocks arrived.

Blackthorns in the hedge were weather lore trees. In autumn they would be blued down with heavy *slah* (sloe), ready for the Saxons to take after a good frosting but in spring they watched the blossom. If it was cold and frosty when the blossom opened it

would stay that way, as 'a blackthorn winter', to the detriment of good seed germination. When it warmed and the blossom fell then it was time to sow.[3] The lore stands up to scrutiny, since the petals fall after pollination and the insects only venture out to do that when the frost period is at an end for a while.[4] Insects love it when the sun throws back its cloudy cloak and beams warmth into the soil again. Soon the hares[5] would be running mad and Saxon children would be just as madly keeping rooks off the fresh sowing. It was a silver-dawn start for them, if they were to beat the birds. At least a good sling shot put meat in the pot. We do not know whether the Saxons harrowed again after sowing to hide some of the seed from the sharp-eyed birds. It would certainly have been wise.

At least cereal seed germinated quickly and was soon rooted into the earth but weed seeds grew just as quickly and would have suppressed the cereals if left unchecked. Out went the Saxons and weeded their fields by hand; what a thankless, back-breaking chore. It was relentless too since the most successful weed-plants over-wintered very happily and flaunted new leaves every clement day. Cornflowers and poppies gave no respite but the worst must have been the corn marigolds since they burgeoned such a mass of smothering leafage so fast. At least they were easy to pull out. Tap-rooted weeds like docks and thistles had to be chipped out with a hand-tool. Presumably a selection of weeds ended up in the cooking pot rather than the midden; certainly many were used in remedies by the herbalists.

So the weeks rumbled on into summer thunder storms and doubtless rituals of supplications to Thunor and the other sky gods, surpassed by those to the sun on the Sunday and then the moon as it passed into the crucial waning stage.[6] Including of course, the moon to grant a quiet time for harvesting. There were daily inspections for fearful blight and other insect infestations, which the Christian monks recorded later in the Anglo-Saxon Chronicles with their Bible term of 'locusts'. Daily inspections monitored the ripening too, until finally, all portends being well, or fear over-riding, they arose one morning to take up their reaping hooks and head for the cornfields.

At their approach flocks of *ceaffince* (chaffinch) would whir up from the grain to alight in line along the hurdle tops that kept out the livestock. The fuss-pot *dopfugel* (moorhen) would stop tip-toeing through the dew at the field-edge and squawk back to the stream-side. Into the corn would wade the reapers.

Reaping would have presented two different scenes in the fields. In some they would have been using reaping hooks while in others, especially on the Romanised estates, they would have used scythes, which had been a Roman innovation.[7] The scythe did not meet with universal approval, since being a tool of percussion meant the impact of the blade could dislodge the grain from the ears. It scattered on the ground and therefore demanded intensive gleaning. A better option was to scythe it before the grains were fully ripe but then it had to be stooked to finish off, leaving it exposed to changes in the weather. Transferring stooks back to the farmsteads for threshing risked the ripe grains falling but at least they were then in more concentrated areas, say round the loading spot, and could be gleaned more efficiently. Ideally what they needed was corn that did not fall out of the ears at all, which was ultimately what was bred and with it of course developments in threshing.

The second option to imagine in the fields entailed the use of the reaping hook, like a small sickle, that had been in use since the Iron Age.[8] It was not a tool of percussion but a draw-knife. The reaper grabbed a handful of ears in one hand and pulled the stems taut while drawing the tool across them to sever them. It was a slow process but reduced losses to the minimum. The Roman writer, Columella reported that it took a day and a half to reap one *iugurum* of corn in this way.[9]

That leaves the question of the straw. If the hooker took off the heads with half their length of straw (as in the Late Saxon illustration in the Julius Work Calendar) then a tallish stubble remained. This would get trampled later when livestock were turned on to the land but could still have been a nuisance when it came to using the ard. It could have been burnt off so that the ashes returned nutrients, such as potash, to the soil, or, it could have been cut again for other uses such as bedding for man and beast but was probably too short for good thatching. Perhaps, if thatching was envisaged the hooker cut the ears off high up deliberately. Scythers on the other hand could cut low and the problem was carted off to the rick ready for threshing. Then the wildlife reclaimed their territory. The *musere* (mousehawk/kestrel) swung its orbit round to float unseen above the stubble and was joined by the *glioda* (red kite) in their evening keenness for blood. (*Kestrel illus. opp.*)

All these crop variations are likely to have been seen even on a short journey through the Surrey fields, especially those of the Thames Valley which are likely to have been the most varied of all. There was variety too in the cornfields themselves, some having wheat or barley while others had oats or rye. The various types of wheat and barley are not of prime concern here for their differences did not come to the fore until their removal from the landscape for processing and using. Doubtless they tried growing millet too, as it was common on the Continent, but it does not flourish in the English climate and was dispensed with in favour of other cereals.[10] A lot of evidence as to exactly what was grown, and where, comes from funeral services! When the potters made the cremation urns they often got grains of corn stuck in the clay which burnt away during firing but left a permanent recognisable indent. How fortunate that these potters were not obsessed with a clean workspace! Thus the archaeologists excavating at Hawks Hill, Leatherhead, unearthed evidence for types of wheat. Thus by various means we know that the Iron Age people had grown a basic sort of wheat called Einkhorn or Small Spelt but this died out in favour of Large Spelt, with bigger grains and high nutrient value, and that type persisted in agriculture through into Saxon times where it was found, for example, in Canterbury.[11] Otherwise the wheats that came to the fore were the Club Wheat and the Bread Wheat and on occasions different types were grown together as a mixed crop.[12] This need not have been a preferred cropping policy but one that arose out of poor status, when the farmer had to grow whatever was left uneaten or perhaps it had been traded cheaply for being in some way sullied.

Just as varied across the Surrey fields were the types of barley. There were more fields of barley than wheat, not only because the soils in most districts suited barley better (especially on the chalk) but because the barley had two uses: bread and beer. The two options had given rise to separate types: the hulled and the naked. For bread they preferred the naked barley since they did not have to contend with the grains having outer shells whereas the shelled grains of the hulled barley made no difference in the brewing process. Not that barley bread was very wonderful anyway. The grain had to be dried and roasted first, which destroyed most of its gluten content, meaning the dough did not rise like wheat dough and so the bread was heavy with a thick crust. It was greyish to look at and earthy to taste. Being nearly solid carbohydrate made it very sustaining but it was not highly nutritive in that the protein content was low. The rest of the meal had to compensate, which was not a problem if it included meat, fish or beans.[13] There were strong flavours available too. Leeks were very popular because they are winter weatherproof, grew throughout the year and could be used at any stage in their development. There were onions too and garlic, including the wild garlics such as *hramsan* (ramsons). Meals could be very good and tasty. Barley bread was much improved if wheat flour had been mixed in but plain barley bread was deemed low status and the food of the poor. Christians told of Christ feeding the five thousand with barley loaves (New Testament; St. John; 6:9). The Romans had used it as punishment rations for the troops and as slave food. Was it slave food in Early Saxon England too?

If need be, barley could also have been fed

to the livestock in winter. The Romans had a tradition, reported by Columella, that stallions should be fattened on it prior to mating and that it should be fed to mares after foaling, while Pliny had reported it was good for muscle strength. This know-how does seem to have been practised in England judging by the barley preserved in the horse coprolites recovered from Lancaster.[14]

Of course oats are the famous food for horses and that seems to have been started in England by the Romans. Before that the Iron Age people used oats as the basis for their own pottage. The Saxons may well have used them primarily for fodder since archaeological records are more frequent from the countryside than the towns.[15] Nevertheless usage in pottage did not die out. Oats have special nutritive qualities and a distinctive flavour.

It is often debated whether archaeological finds relating to oats could be from Wild Oats as a weed and a contaminant in the fields of different cereals or whether from the distinct cultivated form. To distinguish between the two requires the floret base of the chaff to have

survived. Be that as it may, oats became an established crop in the Iron Age, having arrived late because they came from the east rather than the Mediterranean. Their expansion coincided with that of horsepower, which implies they were always grown as a fodder crop. That was invaluable in Britain because even in wet summers they could still be fed green as fodder, without having to ripen fully. Furthermore, they are the most tolerant cereal of damp, acid soils and there were plenty of those in Surrey. That's just what they had at Oatlands Park but that place-name does not get recorded until 1383 so we can only ponder whereabouts in the lower Wey valley the Early Saxons tilled fields for oats. Indeed the county is almost devoid of cereal place-names from Saxon times, except for Waddington, which derives from *Hwætedune* (wheat hill), recorded about 880.[16]

Lastly, there was rye, which grew some four feet high and therefore looked very different from that grown in Surrey today, which is sprayed with hormone to stunt its growth. That is to avoid the straw problem. Presumably this long, very tough straw was used by the Saxons for thatching and then with the invention of horse collars in the Mid Saxon period came the use as collar stuffing. Otherwise rye was the food of the poor and grown widely in Saxon England, leaving diverse evidence from place-names to pottery indents. The evidence however is for small amounts, as though it were garnered as a weed in the corn rather than being cropped (regularly) in its own right.[17] That would be at variance, surely, with place-names? Furthermore, rye was so important as to have a month named after it, *Rugern*, but only if that word does mean 'rye harvest', which is not certain. If it does, then it opens debate as to which month was intended. Most often it gets ascribed to September which is a bit worrying when, from later times, we know rye in England was cut in July. That gives credence to those who propose it was indeed July, or August. Of course, a July harvest refers to England whereas the Saxon reference (in the preamble to the Laws of the Kentish King Wihtræd c.695) may be using names from a Continental calendar, which may in turn have travelled with the crop out of western Asia. Rye grows fruitfully further north than any other cereal and so an August or September date is not out of the question. One thing is certain, rye grows very well on poor sandy soils and Surrey had square miles of that. Farmers would have looked for sunshine in the third week of January because that foretold a good rye harvest. Later they watched the blackthorn (*illus above)* because the longer it bore its blossom into May the better the rye harvest. If they cut it in July then it was the first of their cereal harvests. Following on was the autumn-sown barley and then the spring-sown barley and then the wheat. It was expecting a lot of the English climate to leave the rain clouds on stand-by for that long.

It is worth remembering that rye was the primary host of the parasitic fungus ergot that produced dark little fruiting bodies among the grains in the ear. Each of the club-shaped fruits held horrendous mind-altering drugs and these had been used by shaman to help them commune with the gods and had been part of the rites of human sacrifice.[18] The Saxons did not want that in their bread.

Harvesting the corn they let light and air back to the soil, triggering the germination of dormant weed seeds while existing weeds, straggling through the crop, took on a new lease of vengeance. One would have been the Chickweed but that was probably gathered to take back home for the poultry. The arable fields or *ersc* (as in Won*ersh*) had their own poultry, such as the *ersc enn* (stubble hen, quail (*illus. top right*) which was very small (7 inches or about midway between a house sparrow and a starling). They

had been hiding in the corn but became noticeable in the stubble, feasting upon the bounty of dislodged insects, pupae and corn. Then they got the fresh salad of emerging weed leaves in the new carpet of *edisc* that gave them the alternative name of *edisc henn.*[19]

It was a pity the quails did not take all the mayweed seed since that was such a smothering weed, suppressing the other fodder without being palatable itself. It has been suggested as the origin of the name Mayford[20] and certainly white swathes of it across the arable by the ford would have been a striking landscape feature on what was probably a notable routeway.[21] That said, it would only have been eye-catching when in flower and even then, for only one year, since that would have been enough to teach farmers to clean it out. Some of the farmers must have been unfamiliar with it since it only became an arable weed during the Roman period (perhaps introduced as a seed contaminant). There are no early references to Mayford for further guidance but Gover *et al* proposed *Mæga's ford* from a personal name, which is the more convincing of the two proposals.[22] Either way, it was a useless weed. At least fat hen and knotweed could be stripped of their seeds for the cooking pot but evidence of 'greens' in the pot relies upon the advanced science techniques of chromatography and GC/mass spectrometry. These identify wax compounds from out of the leaves that got encrusted onto the wall of the clay cooking pot. How amazing that a small piece of broken pot can still tell us what was cooked in it all those centuries ago.

More readily available is evidence in the language. Thus we know that the cursed groundsel weed was known as the *grundeswylige* or 'ground swallower' from the profusion of seedlings that germinated. That, however, is a later Saxon naming. It was a corruption of the earlier *gundeswylge* or 'pus-swallower', which opens eyes into herbal medicines and their poultices for septic wounds. The little boys loving those boar-hunt

stories would not have wanted to dwell upon such traumas. Maybe they encountered the groundsel in their religion, associated with sacred iron, because the tradition still prevails that groundsel must never be weeded out with an iron tool.[23]

Another cornfield weed with sacred associations was the blood-red *popæg* (poppy). The Saxons loved colour and they knew of no other flower in England of such intense redness, massed together on a sunny morning. As though poppy fields were not striking enough the Saxons were mindful that red was the colour of the gods and the poppies must have seemed especially spiritual since the wavelength of the redness upsets perception in the brain, if the flowers are stared at for too long. Therefore poppies occur in those great allegories that explained the demise of fertility through the winter. Sadly, the Saxons did not write down their version but the Roman myth is well known, wherein Ceres' beautiful daughter, Proserpina, attracts the venereal interests of Pluto. Unable to control his lusts he burst out of the Underworld into the cornfield where Proserpina was picking poppies and abducted her to the Underworld. Ceres went frantic. Eventually she traced Proserpina and negotiated with Pluto for her release. She had to strike a compromise. Pluto would allow Proserpina back for six months only, while for the rest of the year she had to return to him. Annually the world went into mourning for six months for the loss of Proserpina's beauty and the grief-stricken Ceres forbade the land to bear fruit. When Proserpina returned Ceres was happy and allowed the land to be fruitful again. Poppies must be left in the cornfields as the seal to the agreement. [24]

Trying to rid the fields of poppies would have been impossible as the seed does not all germinate at the same time. There would always have been a few that popped up when they were not looking! The wonder crop of eddish gave rise to the practice of turning the livestock onto the stubble, often for the night, to graze the problem away and to dung the land. This goes down in history books as 'eating the stubble' but was not really the case, since there was next to no nutritive value in the straw. The animals ate the fresh weeds. That said, the older breeds of livestock did best when a significant percentage of their daily intake was coarse or woody roughage, so some of the straw would indeed have been consumed, without the implication that the livestock were barely surviving.

It is most likely that this practice gave rise to August being known as *weodmonath* (weedmonth). However, 'weed' could mean any plant to the Saxons so it could be misunderstood if viewed solely in terms of the noxious. Bede tells us it had meant the month of 'tares' because they were plentiful then and tares gets translated regularly as 'vetches'. That could be totally misleading, for although the Saxons knew the value of vetches the archaeology has not evidenced enough to make sense of them naming a month. On top of that, 'tares' could mean weeds, in the sense of unwelcome plants. That would certainly have been known to Bede, from a parable in St. Matthew's Gospel (13:24-30). The usual interpretation of that parable does not have 'tares' being vetches but the grass called darnel. That, however, is not present in the archaeological record until later times. However, another name for it was 'cockle' and there is

plenty of material on that but it relates to the corncockle. This makes it look as though 'cockle' was somehow associated with toxic, for the corncockle is laden with poisonous saponins, the darnel was reputedly poisonous and the name was used also for white campion, with poisonous seeds. By the time the Saxons were writing they were calling the corncockle *githrefe, gythrofe* and *githrife,* which looks as though it comes from the Latin, from the 'gith' in the Bible, leaving uncertainty as to what the pagans called them. Whatever its name, it could certainly have dominated weed concerns in August. By then the plant had gone to seed and browned off but harvesters using reaping hooks could miss it out since the seedpods are large urn-shaped structures, clearly distinctive from ears of corn. It was those farmers who used the scythe who ran the greatest risk since the straw-coloured corncockle stems blended beautifully. In the transit from field to threshing yard the seeds would not have bounced out of the pods since they stay attached until winter wet rots away the pod to release the seeds. It was a different matter in the threshing yard, whether the harvest was flailed or trampled by the oxen. Each seed is the size and weight of a grain of corn and so would pass through the sieving, winnowing process and could end up being palmed into the querns. When ground they made the flour greyish, odoured, and toxic. It was a slow poison. It deformed the red blood cells (haemolysis), reducing their capacity to carry oxygen and iron. Debility and anaemia resulted and consumption over a prolonged period resulted in death. Obviously people feeling tired were encouraged to eat more food (bread), which exacerbated the problem. Either they had to pick out the dark brown seeds every day or else dump their precious but contaminated corn. The weed was a curse. It was not British but arrived during the Roman period, implying that it was a contaminant in seed corn from the Mediterranean.[25] (*illus over.*)

An alternative theory about *weodmoneth* centres on the workforce going through the corn to remove nettles and thistles before they savaged the reapers. Allowing thistles to get into the stooks was doubtless unforgivable. It does not sound significant enough to warrant naming a month though. Weeds like those must have been dealt with on a regular basis. Nettles made good fodder, good pot-herbs, important textile fibres and the juice acted as a vegetable rennet to curdle milk for cheese making.[26] Nettles were virtuous

and so were thistles. The new rosettes of leaves could be cut in spring as a pot herb (cooking softened the spines!) while the tap roots unearthed in winter could be eaten also (astringent and stringy!). The pink flowers were gathered as another rennet. The fluffy seedheads made the softest down available, used widely from being the binding material in ointments to making warm linings for baby wrappings. They had to be quick to get the seedheads though for they were a favourite food of the delightful little *pisteltwige*, or thistle tweeker - the goldfinch.

Later, across the stubble, they would spot another little bird, flashing its white rump as it passed through on migration, and that was the wheatear. It had nothing to do with wheat. The name has been 'cleaned up' from the Saxon *hwitars* or white-arse.

Saxons worked hard to garner the gifts of the gods and even after the garnering there was drying, parching and threshing still to do. Even so, that had to wait a while to give time for the harvest celebrations. These were so important that they caused September to be called *halegmonath* (holy month). That, according to Bede, was due to all the sacred rites that were held. As a Christian monk it is not surprising that Bede was interested specifically in religious ritual but *halegmonath* must surely have included much that might be deemed secular. Our thinking needs to be broadened. For one thing the Saxons must have been mindful beyond their own harvests that this was the time when shipping returned to port to tie up for the winter, bringing the last of the summer season's precious imports and even more precious, the family members who had survived the voyages. This would have been a terminal point to the summer's economy. The earliest Saxons in *Londinium* would have been well aware that everything went very quiet on the great river, and so too, in all probability, did succeeding Saxons for it meant the end of messaging between the folks back home. The sharp decline in activity for the winter had been a factor in the local economy for all the Roman period and so Thames-side agriculture was attuned to that. With the departure of the legions things would never be the same again. It was probably devastating to a place like *Ad Pontes* (The Bridges) since later Saxons called it *Stanes* (Staines) meaning the place of stones, as though it had fallen into ruins. They seem to have shunned it for a settlement of their own on the opposite bank (*Egeham*/Egham), with their own wharf or *hythe,* hence Egham Hythe.

If we continue to broaden our view then we need to think beyond corn and other plant produce. Animals were vital too and the spring births would have matured and fattened through a good green summer to be ready for marketing. Saxons did understand that the gene pool needed to be mixed regularly and so autumn cattle markets are to be expected, ahead of the next mating season. What better time or place than adjacent to the temple sites when the people were gathering anyway?

Imagine sheep and goats penned within wattle hurdles as discerning farmers wandered from one to the other. Cattle may well have been tethered to stakes. Horses on the other hand were probably a major feature and relegated to the field-side where boys could ride them up and down to show off fitness while their seniors haggled. The womenfolk could well have been conducting a textile market, trading bolts of cloth for those of rarer colours or holding whitened linen to the sun to show off the purity of the bleaching. Traders offered them everything from powdered dyes and sewing needles to glittering brooches and pendants. We know from the grave goods how the women liked to dress in their best and show off their jewellery, to the pride of the menfolk, and these markets would account for the rapid spread of new fashions. Indeed these meetings must have been crucial in spreading all the new ideas, whether in fashion or agriculture or technology. Similarly, with whole communities drawn together this would have been a prime time to hold courts and to adjust laws and administration. It would have been a bit cold and dark if they had left it all to the great midwinter celebrations.

Going back to the rituals, it is not known what the celebrations entailed and most writers leave it at that but a few things can be said or deduced. They did not engender outrage to later Christian writers, like Gildas and Bede, who pass over them rather than denounce them, or to Church leaders who would later preach against them. The thanksgiving was common to both faiths and does not sound as though it was fundamentally different. The Christians in Surrey knew ancient Judaic practice from the Old Testament, from the *Book of Exodus* (written c.1300-1400 BC when England was in its Bronze Age). Ancient though it was, it influenced all succeeding periods and instructed that, "*Three times thou shalt keep a feast unto me in the year*...[firstly the Passover]..*and the feast of harvest, the first fruits of thy labours, which thou hast sown in the field: and the feast of ingathering, which is in the end of the year, when thou hast gathered in thy labours out of the field.* (*Exodus 23, 14-16; repeated 34:22 specifying the wheat harvest*).

It is also unlikely that there were issues over the principle of holding the rites at a temple for that too was endorsed: "*The first of the firstfruits of thy land thou shalt bring unto the house of the Lord thy God." (Exodus 23, 26).*[27]

Although there must have been arguments as to whether there was one god or a pantheon of gods, the basic celebration of the harvest was perpetuated by the Christians, with the first fruits (the first stook of cut corn) being taken to church for a special 'loaf mass'. That name got corrupted into 'lammas'. It was so important that the communal cornfields would become known as the 'lammas lands'. Those at Godalming survive still.[28]

What does not survive is the evidence to prove that they plaited a 'corn dolly' out of the straws of the last stook to embody the spirit of fertility for carrying over to the next year. That is a modern myth, perpetuated by publishers aware that there is a market for such texts. The error is now exacerbated by numerous websites.[29] So much practice appears to have originated in the Middle East but the Judaic rites described in the *Old Testament* make no mention of such devices. Indeed the notion of trying to keep a sample of the god's goodwill for future benefit is a totally alien concept to the religion, just as it

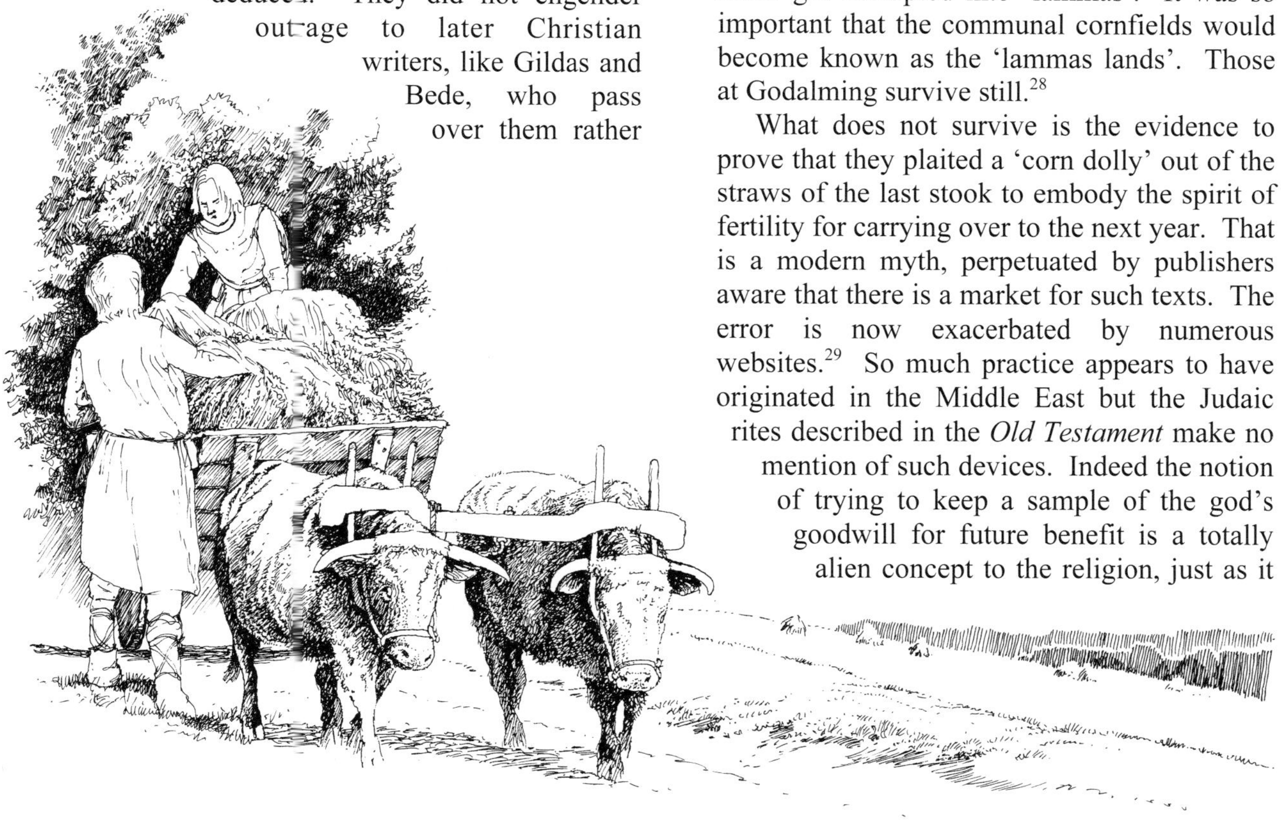

would be to Christianity. There are no admonishments in the Old Testament to shun the harvest practices of the gentiles either.

However, the nature of the rites did change, as the New Testament superseded the Old, which becomes apparent from lines in *Leviticus: "When ye be come into the land which I give unto you, and shall reap the harvest thereof, then ye shall bring a sheaf of the firstfruits of your harvest unto the priest: and he shall wave the sheaf before the Lord, to be accepted for you: on the morrow after the sabbath the priest shall wave it. And ye shall offer that day when ye wave the sheaf an he lamb without blemish of the first year for a burnt offering unto the Lord." (Leviticus 23:9-12).*

Sacrificing animals and burnt offerings link with the next month of the pagan Saxon calendar, which was *blodmoneth* or blood month. That, according to Bede, was the month of sacrifices. That was real blood-letting, until Christianity converted people into accepting a symbolic sacrifice, at the Eucharist. Doubtless there were qualms over accepting this new theology since sacrifice, both animal and human, had been traditional for thousands of years. There is some evidence, from differing periods, that when it involved people they went to their deaths willingly and their experience was tempered by them being drugged beforehand.[30] Death was but a transition from this world to the other world. It was not final so it was not feared. The fear of death came in with Christianity and threats of eternal damnation in the fires of hell.[31]

Both these theologies, pagan and Christian, were practised across the Surrey landscape during the 5th and 6th centuries, with each celebrating the garnering of another harvest. During those celebrations they were doubtless mindful of the need to get back to work quickly if they were planning an autumn sowing. The ard was checked over for worthiness; assurances were given by the oxherd that motive power was ready; boys were anticipating their rite of passage into becoming ploughmen; seed corn was checked for quality and quantity; the moon was watched. Corn was bread and bread was food. When it came to learning the New Testament there was such poignancy in the plea, "*urne gedæghwamlican hlaf syle us to dæg"*

"Give us this day our daily bread".

Left - Corn that the Saxons grew: far left is spelt and to its right is club wheat with the ear in reality being 3.5cm excluding the awns. The spelt ear is 13cm excluding awns. With thanks to Grace Corne for providing the samples.

Above - wild oats, which Saxons grew or else harvested as a weed in other cereal crops.

END NOTES

1 The waxing and waning of the moon is a Saxon expression (*wæx/wana*). To explore lunar planting start with the calendar of Hesiod. That was picked up by Columella whose work probably influenced Romanised estates in Surrey. For help understanding lunar agriculture I am indebted to Vanessa Jones. I was concerned that the principle might not fit the later standardisation of the Christian calendar whereby oats and barley were to be sown on St. David's Day (1st March). She replied, "*In 2008 the 1 March is indeed in the waning phase of the moon as it was in 2003 but in 2007 1 March fell just 3 days before the full moon and would have been a perfect date if you were following lunar/biodynamic principles. Similarly in 2006 1 March was Ash Wednesday just after the new moon so the moon was on the wax again and in 2004 again 1 March was in the waxing phase. As the full moons move around the date calendar sometimes 1 March will be favourable from a lunar planting perspective and sometimes not.*" So our earlier people should have been more successful by following direct observation of lunar movements than later peoples with fixed dates from a standardised calendar. To avoid confusion between the waxing and the waning she added the following *aide memoire* : "*An easy way of telling if the moon is waxing (getting bigger and moving up to the full moon) is to look at it and if it looks like a D then it is waxing and if it looks like a C then it is waning (getting smaller and moving to the new moon). I remember by D = developing and C= contracting. Another way is to think if the illuminated crescent is on the left (the C shape) it is waning and if on the right (the D shape) then it is waxing.*"

2 Agasses, as a Surrey dialect word was still in use in the 1960s but is out of use now and seems to be all but forgotten.

3 Recorded later as:
When the sloe tree is as white as a sheet
Sow your barley, whether it is fine or wet.
And
When the blackthorn's blossom's white
Sow your barley day and night.

4 Surviving weather lore is 'traditional' and it is unknown whether this particular example was known to the Early Saxons but taking everything into consideration makes it a very high contender. Today there is confusion because the white blossom that can emerge in February and gets called blackthorn is not the true *Prunus spinosa,* but *Prunus cerasifera,* introduced in 1880 and now naturalised. The true blackthorn blossoms a little later, in March. For modern grain the spring sowing date is as soon after 20th February as weather permits.

5 Brown hares might have been an introduced species but thousands of years before the Saxon period by when they were well established, not only in the real landscape but also the allegorical landscape of the religions.

6 The language of the waxing and the waning of the moon has devolved down to today from those pagan Saxon worshippers.

7 Alcock p.18.

8 Alcock p.18.

9 Alcock p.18.

10 Hagen (1995) pp 20-1.

11 Hagen (1995) pp.20-1.

12 Hagen (1995) pp.20-1.

13 see Alcock p. 30.

14 From Alcock p.18.

15 Hagen (1995) p.24.

16 Gelling and Cole p.75.

Corn cut, beaten the rain

17 See Hagen (1995) p.25.

18 To explore pagan sacrifice in its context see Grigsby. The Christian Church used mind altering drugs as incense, albeit requiring quite long exposure, but that is just what they had to enable performance of the medieval service of excommunication.

19 Quails today are a scarce summer visitor in Surrey, to farmland north of the scarp of the Downs. No proven recent breeding record. P.c. Penny Hollow.

20 See Gavin Smith p.48.

21 Gelling and Cole p.72; Gover 98.

22 Gover *et al* p.158

23 The smith had been a crucial figure in the allegories for thousands of years. To reach this cultural thread try starting with Wayland the Smith. Iron had a significant role in the rites of the Norse god Thor and it is presumed that these were mirrored in those of his Germanic counterpart, Thunor. Archaeological evidence for metallurgy at this period is still scant.

24 People still believe poppies should be left and when I surveyed this in Surrey in 1985 the prevailing reason was "for the good of the land."

25 Corncockle remained a serious problem for centuries and can be traced through the Surrey farm account books by way of payments to women for picking them out or 'cockling'.

26 The cheese was green and nettles are used still in cheese-making, e.g. Cornish yarg cheese.

27 See also Deuteronomy 26 1-12. Bible translations from the Authorised Version.

28 Other Surrey lammas lands that have public access include the recreation ground at Staines, Chertsey Meads and Woking's Broadmead. Others have been built over but commemorated in road names—see a Surrey street atlas.

29 The history of this myth has been explored afresh by Veronica Main in 'Corn Dollies: Searching for the Seed of Truth' in *Folk Life;* Volume 37 1999 pp 44-63. She includes an assessment of the 'evidence' from Ancient Egyptian tomb paintings. I am indebted to Ruth Wylie for sharing her great knowledge on this issue.

30 As an introduction to this theme, within the wider context of the allegories try Grigsby.

31 That, however, was a misunderstanding of the faith. Nowhere in the Bible did it say that unrepentant sinners would burn in hell or live eternally in its supposed inferno. It did say there would be a lake of fire at the end of the world (Book of Revelation 20:10) but not that sinners dying before that should end up there, nor that sinners would endure an inferno for eternity. What the Bible said was that the punishment for sin would be death, meaning there would be no afterlife and that eternal life was a gift from God not an inevitability. (New Testament. Romans 6:23).

PEAS, BEANS AND LEEKS

The scent of the beanfields when they were in bloom would have been a delight on an evening stroll between the plots. Presumably the Early Saxons did take a few minutes at the end of the day to walk along the dividing baulks and check the progress of crops and weeds. They grew 'field beans' or 'horse beans' which were of the broad bean type.[1] These, together with peas, were both well established crops since they had arrived out of the east, along with barley, back in Neolithic times.

Peas have been bred into two divisions: the small, purple-flowered 'field pea' that still grows wild in Georgia, and the larger, white-flowered form that has become the 'garden pea' of today but for which the wild ancestor appears extinct. Presumably the purple-flowered field pea was commonest but peas of any sort leave little trace in the archaeological record. This scarcity of evidence has led some people think that the Early Saxons grew peas hardly at all. That's highly unlikely since they are so versatile. Both crops gave two returns., not just the seed but also the haulm. Even in a bad year the haulm could be used green as fodder, or, if it could be dried, fed to the animals as per hay. The bean haulm dried much more coarse and woody than the pea haulm but would have suited the goats. The word haulm comes from *halm,* which to the Saxons could mean straw, and that may hint at other uses, especially as the verb 'to haulm' can mean to lay out straight as per straw for thatching. Certainly there are records for pea haulm thatching from the later Middle Ages.

It's hardly surprising that the Romans had continued the Iron Age practice of growing them, simply because they would grow. Other Roman culinary delights, such as the related lentils, found English summers too cold and wet. The Romanised estates would have continued growing them into the 5th century but doubtless they were grown widely beyond these estates. The seeds must have been valued highly simply because they could be dried and kept for the lean time. Their uses were versatile too, from adding them to the pottage to grinding them into meal for thickening the pottage or into flour for baking, whether in the bread dough or baked on hot stones. It looks as though some pulses were used fresh, if that is what was meant by a later reference to *geseawe peas* (juicy peas).[2] Surplus beans could be fed to the livestock, especially horses.

It makes no sense to suggest peas declined in the Early Saxon period. Indeed, with the expansion of Christianity they are likely to have increased, for they were a good source of protein for the Lenten fast when there were Church prohibitions on eating animal protein. It was the Church, however, that had reservations about pulses. They are notorious for what Hagen puts so nicely as, “involuntary bodily functions, including flatulence….” At this point some readers may wish to skip the rest of this paragraph which concerns ‘rudeness’. As noted already, we don’t know exactly how the Saxons swore but we do get a bit of information about their social standards. Specifically, it was the Church that took exception to flatulence, seeing it as a sign of man’s fall from grace. Thus St. Jerome (c.347-420) forbade nuns to have beans because he said they would “tickle the genitals” (*in partibus genitalibus titillationes*).[3] This move towards ‘polite’ behaviour may well have been one of the little ways used by the Christians to exert superiority, just as they came to frown upon swearing. Oaths were directed towards the gods and came within the ambit of blasphemy. Today’s collection of ‘rude’ words is attributed to a Saxon origin,

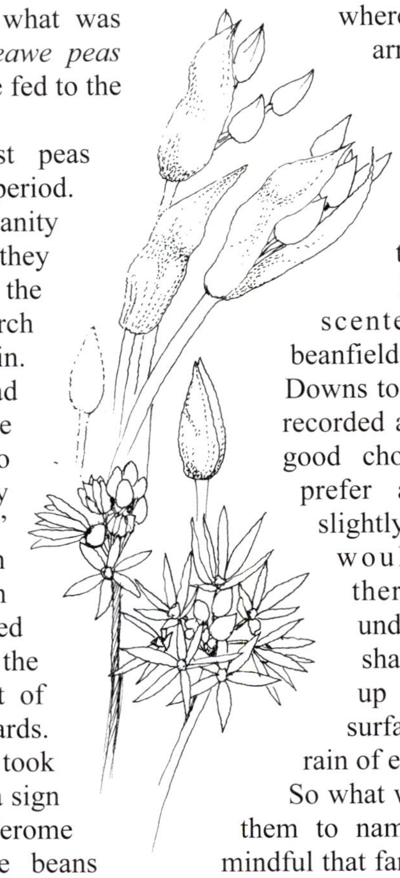

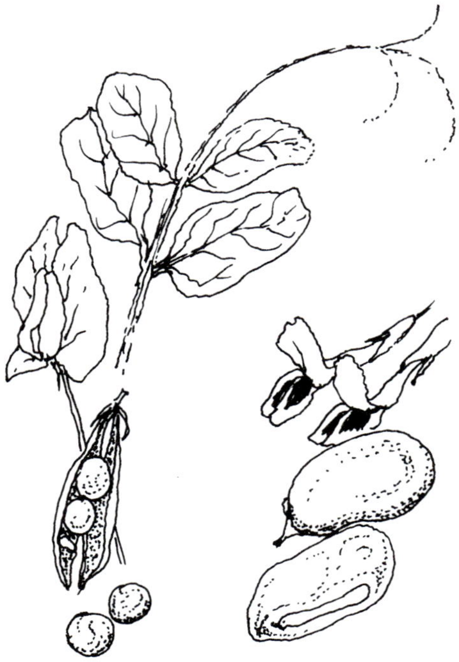

whereas in fact nearly all of them arrived in the language in the Later Middle Ages. An exception is ‘fart’. The OED have not traced an Old English source for this but have been able to back-track to a proposed verb **feortan.*

Returning to a sweetly scented ramble through the beanfields, we could go up on the Downs to Banstead, or ‘bean farmsted’, recorded as *Benstede* in 675.[4] It was a good choice of crop because beans prefer a free-draining, neutral or slightly alkaline soil[5] which is what would have predominated thereabouts. Although the underlying chalk is alkaline the shallow working of the ard stirred up little of this, leaving the surface to become leached in the rain of excessive calcium.

So what was so special at Banstead[6] for them to name the place? It makes me mindful that farms became organised to share responsibility for hosting their overlord and so perhaps Banstead people took responsibility for his beans, or, that beans became the tribute demanded of them. We shall never know. Even the site of their settlement is unknown. Only ten villages of the period have been located[7] but from that small sample it looks as though a hill-top site, such as on the Banstead Downs, would be an option, even if it meant lugging water up from the valley every day.[8]

Although there is no evidence to suggest the Early Saxons drank a lot of pure water, they needed it for making beer and mead. Then there was cooking, cleaning and washing, and for processes such as dyeing. If they repaired there own metalwork then it was needed at the forge. Early Saxons had no less need of water than anybody else and they sank wells to get it. However, not all the references to a ‘well’ should be interpreted in this way. The word was used for all manner of water sources, both running and still, before the word got refined to mean the source they created for greatest convenience. They fashioned wooden pails for carrying it and presumably used animal skins too, which certainly reduced the weight.[9] Water-carrying is another image to add to our overall picturing of the Early Saxon landscape.

Cereals and water are not very flavoursome so the Saxons sought out all manner of strong flavours from the wild, such as *hramsan* (ramsons)(*illus. opp.*) and other wild garlics. At home. they grew onions but their chief plant was obviously the leek since by later Saxon times the term for a vegetable garden was a leek yard. That certainly tells us that gardening was underway as a yard was an enclosed space but how early they started creating gardens remains unknown. Certainly the Roman examples did not inspire their maintenance so it looks as though the practices had to be re-introduced and on the whole that was through emissaries of the Christian Church. Thus in the leek yards other special plants would have been grown too, from medicinals to sacred plants. At West Stow they reported that the archaeologists had looked for evidence of gardens and found none but they might not have left any evidence. Francis Pryor once excavated a known hedge site to find out what difference it had made in the soil and he could detect none. If whole hedges can disappear without trace then it is not surprising that a few rows of leeks could do the same.

Although it might sound unlikely today, leeks were the obvious choice for the main vegetable because they could be gathered throughout the year. The whole green plant was used and so there was no waiting for fruition and when other things failed in a wet season the good old leeks did even better. They were the safest crop for another reason, based upon all members of the onion family having antibiotic properties. Thus their presence in the pot, that was not boiled every day, must have saved countless Saxons from food poisoning.

Other strong flavours, gathered from the wild, served the same purpose and were used also in brewing to extend the life of the beer. Bitter flavour and pungent foliage so often indicates antibiotic qualities that will combat germs but in some cases the action was so powerful as to kill the consumer too. Deadly nightshade and henbane belie their toxicity with pungency (as do potato and tomato plants). Saxons took their chances. They wanted the strong flavours because the pottage and bread would be bland and monotonous without them. However, when whole families are found together in cemeteries from time to time, without showing signs of violence, and when archaeologists ponder the cause of death food poisoning should be high on the list; hemlock waterdropwort isn't called dead man's oatmeal for nothing.

END NOTES

1 Other types of bean were not available until after the discovery of the New World.

2 Hagen (1995) p.38.

3 Hagen (1995) p.38. She sources McGee (1986) p.257 but the full reference has been omitted from the Bibliography.

4 Gover p.68.

5 Tolerates alkalinity up to pH7.0 according to Royal Horticultural Society.

6 There is also Bandon Hill, to the north east in Wallington that might derive its name similarly but other Surrey 'bean' names are only attested far later, such as Benhilton in nearby Sutton.

7 According to Channel 4 *Time Team* 2008.

8 On most chalk downs the water table could have been too far down to reach by well but that might not have been the case at Banstead where the old village well is still preserved.

9 Hagen (1995) has a whole chapter (pp.195-203) on water supply, including 61 bib. refs. For wells in the place-name context see ch.1 in Gelling & Cole (pp1-35).

Magpie fledglings; Saxons called the bird 'agu'.

FIBRES AND COLOURS

Not only was the scent of bean fields a delight but so was the massed flowering of the flax. On a bright day the petals reflected the light and shimmered in the breeze while on cloudbound days the sky-blue petals spread a better day across the land. Possibly the Saxons grew the white-flowered cultivar but the petal colour does not leave an archaeological record. The crop can be traced back to Neolithic times and was always important for being dual purpose, providing both textile fibres and edible seed, rich in oils.

With lengthening days came the rituals to purify the land of evil forces ready for all the seed sowing (Christianised as the Feast Day of the Purification of the Blessed Virgin Mary ; 2nd February) and then with the warming of the soil came the frantic efforts to sow all the season's crops, including flax, before the weather swung cold again. How lean and exhausted they must have been after that phase, with all the crops being sown broadcast. Once Christianity prevailed it became worse when Easter was early and the seed sowing ran into the Lenten fast. The children were running up and down too, keeping the birds off the seed.

Where the seed had fallen sparsely each plant had more room and produced flowering side-stems, increasing the seed yield. Where the seed had fallen more thickly the plants were too close for branching and bolted a single stem towards the light, increasing the length of fibre for textiles. Arguably the Early Saxons did not fret over such niceties but left the crop to run to seed, harvested that, and kept the stems for fibre, whatever the grade. Harvesting was probably in July, between hay-making and barley reaping, and was the most hated of the harvests. It was back-breaking. They had to bend over and grip each plant at its base and pull it up, root and all. Fortunately, at this period, the Saxons were avoiding heavy soils but the job was severe when the plants were concreted into a baked clay soil.

Birds were a menace too. At sowing, the children had to be energetic keeping them off, especially the one that got named after the *lin* crop, the *linete* (linnet). Then, as the crop ripened, they were busy again, keeping off the same bird which was now called a *Linetwige* (flax/lin tweaker).[1]

The plant was called *flex* and must have been a widespread crop in Surrey, where in the dialect it became 'flex' rather than flax, as in Flexlands at Chobham.[2] Then there is the district of Upper and Lower Flexford, east of Ash. That was recorded as 'Flexwere in

Asshe' in 1317 and Gover (p.135) suggests 'flax weir' as the original but offers some later confusions. The idea of a flax weir makes perfect sense, because unknown to Gover was the existence of a complete flax-retting pool at Lower Flexford (the only one I have managed to identify in Surrey; now altered[3]). It was a widening of a stream into a large flat-bottomed pond with a bypass channel for the stream, controlled by sluice-boards, so that the pond could be filled and drained at will. It would have been drained ready for stacking the flax bundles in there before filling it again, so that the water rotted (retted) the outer plant tissue ready for processing the inner fibres. The age of the pond is not known but in Early Saxon times they most likely retted their flax by the different method, known as dew-retting. That entailed spreading the harvest beside a water course and then soaking it, at least once a day, until it was sufficiently rotted for the rest of the processing to commence. That involved a lot of hard labour and could produce uneven retting, even when the flax was forked over each day. Nevertheless, it was another scene out in the fields to add to this overview of the agricultural landscape. It's another smell too, for retting flax can stink and the polluted water antagonises all the other users downstream.

A second textile crop was *henep* (hemp) and that too ran on into the Middle Ages as an important Surrey product. Although it was most likely to have been introduced into this country only in Roman times it is likely that the Saxons perpetuated its use without hesitation because it was versatile. It grew so fast that it can be pulled eighty days after sowing and that left time to crop the land a second time. The poorer the soil the finer the fibres and so that suited their fields when dung was always at a premium. After shifting the dung the midden site could then be cropped with hemp while a new midden was building up; a very useful practice. It could be grown also as small patches in odd corners rather than necessitating field space.

Fine fibres were good enough for clothing while coarse fibres became ropes and sacking but in textiles it looks as though hemp and linen were used interchangeably. Tracking this crop through pollen analysis is not possible since hemp pollen is indistinguishable from that of the hop.[4]

They did have a third option for fibres and that was the *netel.* Stinging nettles yield really good fibres and had been in use for thousands of years. Even the rare survival of a piece of cloth still needs to go under the microscope to distinguish nettle cells from flax cells and so our knowledge of this material for Early Saxon times is scant. All in all it looks as though any usage was probably by gathering from the wild. Wild nettles have left their record. One of the islands in the Thames at Chertsey (since removed) was called *Netelyge* in 675.[5]

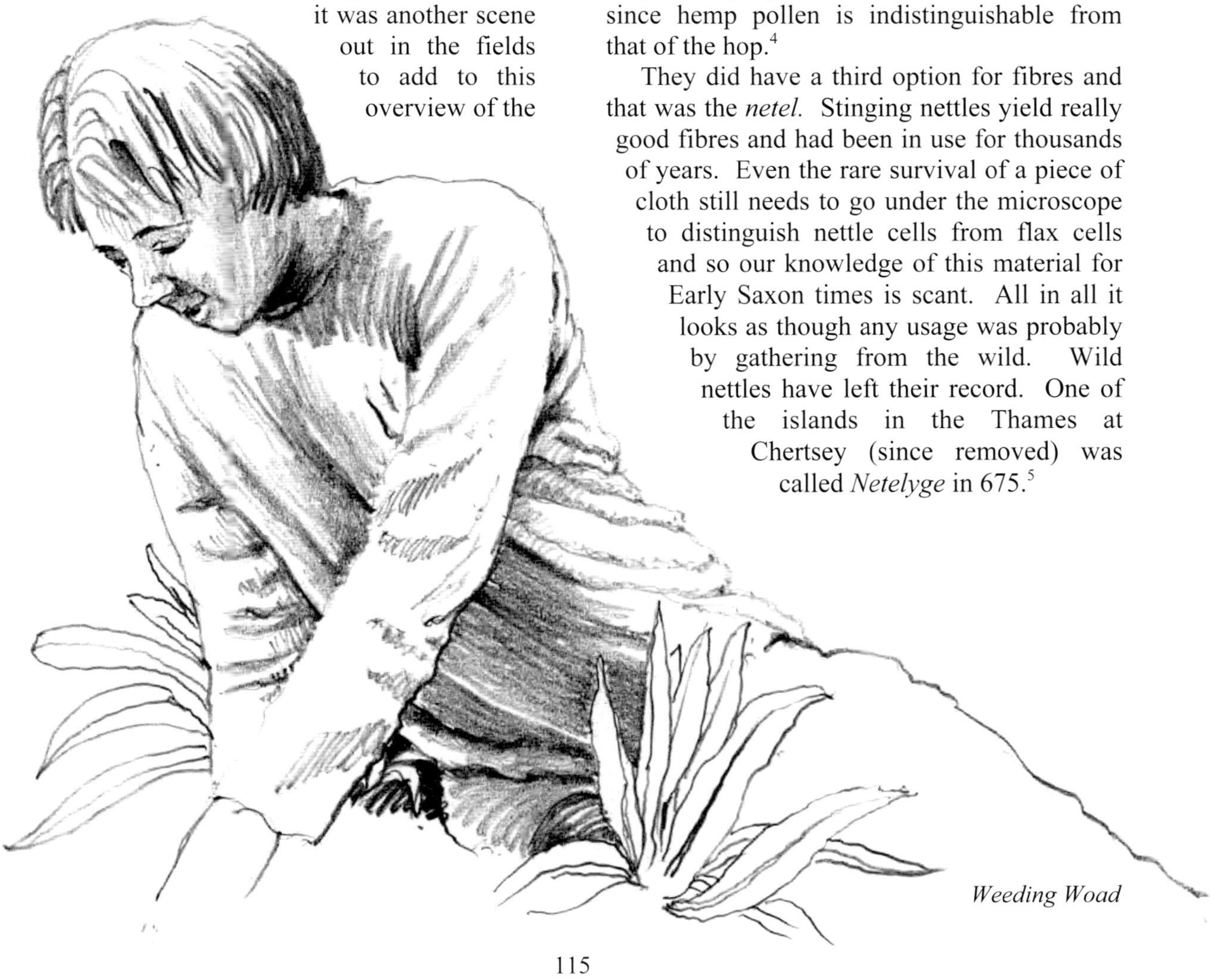

Weeding Woad

Retting pool, Flexford as it was in 1990.

Turning now from the fibres to the dyes that coloured it and the famous one is the woad, from the Old English *wad,* although the earliest surviving records of the name are from Norman times.[6] The *wad* plant was of exceptional importance for yielding blue dye, and a strong solution gave a very good blue at that. Ultimately it faded lighter and sometimes greyer. Most usefully it could be mixed with yellow dye to give a quality green. Records from all over North West Europe suggest that the blue and the green were the universal colours that we should imagine being worn by the workers in the fields.

The plant had been in use since Late Iron Age[7] and so its cultivation was of ancient knowledge. They grew it from seed, when the strengthening sun started to warm the soil again and soon there would be rosettes of long-stalked lanceolate leaves of a distinctive greyish green so that even the children could be trusted to weed the patch without removing the wrong plants. It was the leaves that were harvested as the dye source and they were ready in about ten weeks. Whether they left the plants to recover and so get a second harvest is unknown. What is certain is that a few plants were left to grow on into their second year, ready for flowering, to provide seed for the future. For that the plant bolted up a tall stem 120cm high that branched out into twiggy heads bearing bright yellow flowers, so that although each bloom was very small (4mm) there were so many that several plants together put on quite a show. If there were specialist growers for producing seed, then their bright yellow fields would have made a striking colour statement in the landscape.

To get a yellow dye, however, different plants were needed and modern science has identified two sources:[8] the wild mignonette called weld[9] and dyers greenweed. Considering how much dye was needed, it seems unlikely that the Saxons could source enough from the wild mignonette, especially as they used the whole plant, taken when in flower (June to August), thereby reducing seeding capacity. Thus it looks highly likely that it was cropped deliberately. It flowers in its second year but maybe they just grew it as an annual to take off the first year leafage only, as per woad. The dyers greenweed is a very different plant, being a shrub of the pea family and a bit like a small broom bush. New growth could have been sheared off and it would have sprouted again, so maybe they could have relied upon wild sources. There was plenty of suitable habitat for it, since it likes rough pastures.

Other colours were possible from British plants but they have not shown up in the limited amount of material available for testing. It looks as though bright colours, often from imported dyes, especially for bright red, were reserved for strips of tablet weave that were sewn on to edges of headdresses, cuffs, etc. to make smart coloured statements. Similarly, it looks as though this native material was collected from the wild, along with herbs for medicines, brewing and cooking, and vegetables for the cooking pot. These are outside the remit of this book but one exception would be the leek.

END NOTES

1 These words may well be later Saxon since they derive from the Latin *linum* which entered the language through the Christian Church.

2 Recorded 1315, Gover 118.

3 The then owner, Mrs J. Turner, and myself tried to ensure this great rarity was preserved but there is no legislation that covers the preservation of a pond.

4 Hops are not included in this review since they would have been gathered from the wild and did not become a crop until the Mid Saxon period.

5 Gover p.111.

6 Gover p.51.

7 Rogers p.37.

8 Rogers p.37.

9 Saxon name not recorded but it is deduced to have been *wealde* and/or *walde*. (OED).

Top - Linnet or 'linetwige'
Below - Corn Bunting, probably called simply 'hrand'.

Early open air prayer meeting

FROM OVER THE SEA AGAIN

There was a day in 597 when the people on a Thanet hythe burst into activity when a ship was spotted heading for port. That was not unusual in the summer months. It was the men on board who proved special. They had set out from Italy under the persuasion of Abbot Gregory of St. Anthony's monastery in Rome, whose powers of persuasion had prevailed since he was also Pope. Being Pope kept him busy so the running of the monastery was left in the hands of their capable and well-educated prior, brother Augustine. It was he who led the mission of about forty brothers to England. They were not happy. On their long journey they had written back to Gregory to ask if they might abort the mission and return home but Gregory told them to get on with it. They must have got off the ship with some relief that the crossing was over, some bemoaning cold, others bemoaning seasickness. The Saxons stood around and stared. Any who had seen Christian monks before had not seen tonsures cut like that. Soon the formalities were over and they were being escorted off (warily) to begin their journey to Canterbury to meet Æthelberht, the most powerful and influential king in the whole of the southern half of England. At least the brothers comforted themselves with the knowledge that his Queen Bertha was a Christian, from the royal house of the Franks who had just been so hospitable (due to letters from the Pope) to the mission as it passed through their lands

They did not bring Christianity to England as is said so often. Bertha was a Christian and she was not alone. Her husband granted personal freedom in matters of religious faith throughout his realm and other kings did the same. The bishops of London have been noted already.

The Christian faith in Early Saxon England was organised through monasteries rather than cathedrals and seven of the bishops turned up at Canterbury to greet the mission but only seven, reported Bede, implying there were more. They were part of the Celtic Church, centred upon Ireland, and they went about their lives quietly without pressuring others unduly to convert to their faith. That was to be the mission's task and pagan Saxons were not going to be converted to Celtic Christianity but to the Roman version and thus it was the Roman Catholic faith that Augustine introduced into England. With it he introduced something else that was just as powerful and that was literacy.

Rural continuity: aerial view of Shalford from above St. Catherine's, from a photo taken by the author in 1988, with the landscape still patterned with field clearings in the trees as it was in Early Saxon times. The 'shallow ford' was over the Tillingbourne rather than the Wey which meanders through the trees right across the view (curve of reflection is directly above this text). The modern church spire has been left in the centre for guidance.

The Roman Church wrote things down so there were no arguments and Augustine soon had King Æthelberht committing the laws of his realm into writing. That was done in the Roman manner, which became the norm for ever after, but there was a crucial difference: the content and the language were specific to Kent, making them the first laws to be written in a Germanic language and the foundation for the corpus of English law, since other kings followed suit. The codes were not a matter of crime and punishment but of crime and compensation, setting out the penalties for conviction of any of the listed offences. Thus the weave of local custom was starched rigid in writing. It starched the lives of the labourers in the fields for ever.

Augustine and his brothers set about evangelising and with great success. The key issue was the guarantee of salvation to all those who died in the belief of Jesus Christ when the pagan religions had no such universal guarantee on offer. Famine and disease were constant reminders of their mortality so this news must have swept across the border into Surrey. With Canterbury to the east and London to the north it is easy to imagine that Surrey was soon evangelised. That is not supported by the evidence. So far, the archaeology of early Christianity in Surrey is almost absent. Even when place-names are reviewed there are only a couple of interest, such as St. Martha's at Guildford (*illus. below*), if it derived from 'martyrs'.[1] That leaves commentators observing that Surrey must have been one of the last bastions of paganism, especially the south western quarter.

It was from the edge of this quarter, at Godalming, that the site of a very early Christian church was discovered and excavated in the 1860s. It was up on the hill at Tuesley (now under the garden of Tuesley Court), where the temple of Tîw was converted to the new faith and a little church built. That became a minster or mother church,[2] with daughter churches to follow as evangelists spread their mission out into the district. It was superseded by the building of a bigger church in the valley where the settlement of Godalming was growing apace. Part of that Saxon church is still embodied in the present one.

When exactly the Tuesley church was established is unknown (7th century) and so it is not possible to fit it with certainty into the sequence of conversions. It need not have derived directly from Augustine's mission but from a later expansion and so some commentators wonder about Dorchester on Thames, over in Oxfordshire. The handsome riverside village of today was formerly of far greater importance. The Iron Age people built a hill fort there, provoking the Romans into building a walled town that persisted after the Romans left, with archaeological evidence that this became an important settlement for the Early Saxons. Here in the 630s came a Roman monk called Berinus, better known by his Latinised name Birinus. He had been consecrated bishop by the Archbishop of Milan under instruction from Pope Honorius I but was not given a diocese. Instead he was dispatched on a conversion mission to create a new one and that brought him to England. As he travelled on into the pagan Midlands he reached Dorchester, in the kingdom of Wessex, and met its pagan King Cynegils. Also present was Oswald, the Christian king of Northumbria. Birinus converted Cynegils and baptised him, uniting two of the greatest kingdoms in a common faith,[3] spliced by Cynegils marrying the daughter of Oswald. To Birinus Cynegils gave land for a cathedral and from that little wooden church Birinus created a vast diocese, stretching from Hampshire to Yorkshire. It therefore had a border with Surrey. Right on that border is Farnham, where another one of Surrey's very early churches was established and that is why some commentators look towards Dorchester as possibly the significant locus.

To what extent conversion changed the everyday lives of the people in the fields is conjectural. We do not know how the pagans venerated their deities on a day to day basis but such a daily basis was almost certainly in place since the most important gave their names to days of the week, such as Tîw on Tuesday. Bearing in mind that most of them lived and worked in isolated groups, miles from the main temples, it would seem likely that whatever observances were practised were private devotions at home. Under early Christianity (before all the saints' days were added) the emphasis shifted to one Sabbath, on what had been the Sun's day. For this they were encouraged to travel to a church to worship collectively. No example of a wooden church of the Early Saxon period has survived in Britain but it used to be thought that the timber church at Greenstead-juxa-Onga, in Essex, might date from the end of the Mid Saxon period. Then dendrochronology comparison of the timbers in the 1960s established the date 845, until further scientific tests in 1995 adjusted that to about 1053 and not later than 1108. Of course some of the timbers may have been reused from earlier churches on the site and under the chancel floor they found the remains of two little wooden buildings that might take the site back to the late 6th or early

7th century. Of course we do not know whether those were for Christian or pagan usage (St. Cedd began converting the East Saxons about 654). Whatever the dates, the present church leaves no doubt as to the superiority of craftsmanship in timber in those far off days.

Oddly, the nave walls are low whereas Saxon churches in general had high walls. Of course, high walls might have been reduced by removing decayed timbers ends at the last rebuild. Those high walls are what we see in Surrey at Wisley Church (*illus. top left*) although the workmanship is Norman. That suggests that the Normans built round the Saxon church (to save rebuilding the roof) and then took out the decayed Saxon one (as happened elsewhere in England). Thus the Normans retained unavoidably the Saxon proportions. When compared with the Norman church of the same date in the next parish of Pyrford (*illus. bottom left)* the differences are striking, with Pyrford looking long and low, for the new processional services. The best thing about Wisley is not what is there but what is missing - later developments. The site is still a huddle of church, manor house and farm (recently redeployed) beside the river amid the Surrey greenery. As a design idea it is still the same as when the first Christian Saxon leaders created their communities.

That can be seen again, some miles off, at Wanborough (*illus. below*) where the chapel (13th century), manor house, and farm buildings huddle together below the north scarp of the Hog's Back with farmland all around. Although the buildings are later it is the design that echoes Saxon times, when the pagans passed through here to the Wanborough temple, a few minutes' walk away.

For a third example go to Stoke D'Abernon where the late Saxon stone church survives adjacent to the manor house (rebuilt in Georgian times) on the banks of the Mole.

Thus the grouping of church, manor and community was the foundation of a new-look England that persisted till the present. settlements became villages; villages became towns and even today Surrey's towns still have evidence of Saxon times. Hidden, unseen by the public, in the core of Godalming's church is walling from the early stone version. Available for all to see, is the late Saxon tower of St. Mary's in Quarry Street, Guildford (*illus. left*)

END NOTES

1 Gavin Smith offers the longest list, which is inevitably controversial and all the more interesting for that.

2 For more details see Malden; *Victoria County History:* Surrey, vol. III, p.41.

3 The significance is that once the king changed faith the rest of his people would have done the same. For an explanation of that see Chaney.

LAST WORDS

As the Saxon farmers trudged in from the dusky fields feeling the job was done so it feels the same for having reached the end of the book. Farmers and writers always know a few tasks have been left undone and others could have been done better but time moves on relentlessly. Different seasons threw up new challenges to Saxon farmers just as each new season of archaeology yields fresh information. A book like this will never be 'finished' and there will never be definitive answers to so many of the imponderables. Exploring the varying suggestions and proposals is all part of the fascination with this period and all the statements in this book have derived from historians and archaeologists, although they will not agree with each other on all issues! Sadly, for lack of space, some of the vast topics have been put aside, like home-life, going to market and the specialist craftsmen, from the woodworker to the blacksmith. Thankfully the Saxons gave us the salvation of an expression - *to morgenne* - tomorrow!

Those far off people gave a fresh identity so quickly to the 5th and 6th centuries and laid enduring foundations for a future nation. They fed and nurtured the disparate into new kingdoms that would unite by conquest into a common culture with a common language. That was not 'subsistence' farming; that was achievement. Through all that they have left us, we feel the touch of real people, tracing their way along the life lines of the palms into which they bequeathed the land. They are people we can recognise and with whom to have a rapport, with whom we can pause to enjoy a kingfisher or a lapwing, fear the wolf or the onset of harvest rain. We can hear the groans of the weeders in the fields when they straightened their backs and looked out across their fields. Those were the heroes just as much as the warriors they sustained, so that at the end of *Beowulf (ll 3007-3027* Heaney*)* when the warriors gave honourable burial to their great leader and recited the eulogies, there is a poignant line that implies he had never lost the common touch but joined in heartily with evenings of mead and mirth, for it says quite simply that their leader's laugh was now silenced.

FURTHER READING

As this book was not intended as a textbook for archaeologists each statement has not been footnoted in the final version since it produces too many pages of archaeology reports. Readers are referred specifically to the long bibliographies in the two books by Ann Hagen for agriculture, etc. and for the range of other topics see the bibliography in Donald Henson.

General Introductions

For the preceding period as background, a fresh approach comes from Guy de la Bédoyère, such as

De la BEDOYERE, Guy (2006); *Roman Britain: a New History; Thames and Hudson.*

MATTINGLEY, H. and HANDFORD, S. A. (eds.) (1970); *Tacitus: The Agricola and the Germania;* Penguin Classics

PRYOR, Francis (2003); *Britain BC;* HarperCollins [runs into Romano-British times]

PRYOR, Francis (2004); *Britain AD;* Harper Collins.

The two above are very readable and valuable for concentrating upon people rather than brooches and bits of pot. He gets converted from the migration theory to acculturation between the two books. For the aftermath there is:

PRYOR, Francis, (2006); *Britain in the Middle Ages;* HarperCollins.

General surveys of Early Saxon times:

ALCOCK, L. (2001); *Arthur's Britain: history and archaeology AD 367-634;* Penguin Books Ltd.

ARNOLD, C. J. (1997 2nd ed.); *An Archaeology of the Early Anglo-Saxon Kingdoms;* Routlege. Does not include agriculture despite a chapter headed 'Farm and Field'.

CHANCY, William A. (1970); *The Cult of Kingship in Anglo-Saxon England: the transition*

from paganism to Christianity; Manchester University Press.

DARK, K. R. (2000); *Britain and the End of the Roman Empire*; NPI Media Group.

GLASSWELL, Samantha (2002); *The Earliest English: Living and Dying in Anglo-Saxon England;* Tempus. Very readable and has valuable colour plates of reconstructed costume.

HAYWOOD, John (1991); *Dark Age Naval Power: Frankish & Anglo-Saxon Seafaring Activity ;* Routledge Very informative/interesting.

HENSON, Donald (2006);*The Origins of the Anglo-Saxons*; Anglo-Saxon Books. Very valuable as he sets out the conflicting theories and cites the key texts for each. Very wide ranging content.

HIGHAM, N. (1992); *Rome, Britain and the Anglo-Saxons*; Routledge.

HILLS, C. (2003) *Origins of the English*; Gerald Duckworth & Co Ltd.

HINES, J. (ed.) (1997); *The Anglo-Saxons from the Migration Period to the Eighth Century: An Ethnographic Perspective*; Boydell Press

MORRIS, J. (1989); *The Age of Arthur: A history of the British Isles 350 -650*; Weidenfield and Nicolson.

MYERS, J. N. L. (1988); *The English Settlements*; Oxford.

POLLINGTON, Stephen (2003); *The Mead-Hall: Feasting in Anglo-Saxon England;* Anglo-Saxon Books. Covers the whole Saxon period. Wide ranging content from architecture to etiquette.

YORKE, Barbara (1990); *Kings and kingdoms of Early Anglo-Saxon England;* Routlege. Primarily genealogical, including Surrey's neighbours.

Costume

ROGERS, Penelope Walton (2007); *Cloth and Clothing in Early Anglo-Saxon England, AD 450-700;* Council for British Archaeology (Research Report 145).

Food and Agriculture

ALCOCK, Joan (2002); *Food in Roman Britain;* Tempus. Useful for continuity

BRIGDEN, Roy (1998); *Ploughs and Ploughing;* Shire Publications

COMBE, I. (1987); *Herding Dogs: Their Origins and Development in Britain;* Faber and Faber

DICKSON, Adam (1788); *The Husbandry of the Ancients*; 2 vols; Dickson and Creeca, Edinburgh

GOSSET, A. (1911); *The shepherds of Britain: Scenes from a Shepherd's Life*; Constable and Co.

HAGEN, Ann (revised 1998 ed.); *A Handbook of Anglo-Saxon Food: Processing and Consumption;* Anglo-Saxon Books

HAGEN, Ann (1995); *A Second Handbook of Anglo-Saxon Food and Drink: Production and Distribution*; Anglo-Saxon Books

The two HAGEN books above invaluable, especially for their bibliographies.

HANCOCK, David (1999); *Old Farm Dogs;* Shire Publications

HOWKINS, C. and SAMPSON, N. (2000); *Searching for Hornbeam*; Chris Howkins pub. Addlestone.

URQUART, J. (1983); *Animals on the Farm*; Macdonald and Co. Ltd.

Literature

CROSSLEY-HOLLAND, Kevin (1980), *The Norse Myths;* Deutsch. Remember this is Norse !

HEANEY, Seamus (trans.) (2000); *Beowulf: A New Verse Translation;* W.W.Norton & Co. Justly famous translation that gives traditional values of the culture.

WINTERBOTTOM, M. (1978); *Arthurian Period Sources: Gildas;* Phillimore.

Place-names

EKWALL, Eilert; (1960); *The Concise Oxford Dictionary of English Place-names*; OUP.

GELLING, Margaret and COLE, Ann (2003); *The Landscape of Place-names*; Shaun Tyas, Stamford.

GOVER, J.E.B., MAWER, A and STENTON, F.M.; (1934) *The Place-names of Surrey*; Eng. Place-name Soc. vol. XI; CUP.

SMITH, Gavin; (2005); *Surrey Place-names*; Heart of Albion Press, Loughborough

Plantlife

BIGGAM, C. P. (ed.); (2003); *From Earth to Art:The Many Aspects of the Plant-World in Anglo-Saxon England*; Rodopi; Amsterdam-New York.

DE CLEENE, M. and LEJEUNE, M. C. (2003); *Compendium of Symbolic and Ritual Plants in Europe*; Man and Culture Publishers, Belgium.

GRIGSON, Geoffrey (1955); *The Englishman's Flora;* Dent.

HARVEY, John (1981); *Mediaeval Gardens;* Batsford.

HOUGH, Carole (2003); *Place-name Evidence*

for Anglo-Saxon Plant Names; paper included in BIGGAM above.

POLLINGTON, S. (2000); *Leechcraft: Early English Charms, Plantlore and Healing*; Anglo-Saxon Books. Includes the Old English texts.

Religion and Lore

BEDE, Venerable; *The Ecclesiastical History of the English People;* trans Bertram Colgrave; Oxford World Classics.

DAVIDSON, H. E. (1993); *The Lost Belief's of Northern Europe*; Routledge.

GRIGSBY, John (2002); *Warriors of the Wasteland: A Quest for the Pagan Sacrificial Cult Behind the Grail Legend;* Watkins. Fascinating insights into the great allegories.

HOWKINS, Chris (1996); *Elder – The Mother Tree of Folklore*; Chris Howkins pub. Addlestone.

HOWKINS, Chris (1996); *Rowan: Tree of Protection*; Chris Howkins Pub. Addlestone.

HOWKINS, Chris (1999); *Trees and People*; Chris Howkins pub. Addlestone.

HOWKINS, Chris (2006); *Oak – The Lightning Tree;* Chris Howkins pub. Addlestone.

HUTTON, Ronald (1991); *The Pagan Religions of the Ancient British Isles;* Blackwell. Only a small amount on Saxons but rest useful background.

Surrey

The main resource is the Surrey History Centre at Woking with its extensive library of books on the history of the county and places within the county. Catalogue available on line. Northern Surrey has been swallowed by Greater London and the history material can be traced through individual Borough websites, some of which are listed on the Surrey County Council website's list of neighbouring archives. See websites of Surrey Archaeological Society and the Surrey Museums Service also.

Of particular interest are Bird and Blair listed below:

BIRD, Joanna and D. G.(1987); *The Archaeology of Surrey to 1540;* Surrey Archaeology Society. Contains valuable paper *Saxon Surrey* by Rob POULTON.pp 197-222.

BLAIR, John (1991); *Early Medieval Surrey: Landholding, Church and Settlement before 1300;* Alan Sutton Publishing Ltd and Surrey Archaeological Society.

MALDEN, H. E. (1900); *A History of Surrey;* Elliot Stock.

MALDEN, H. E. (1911); *Victoria County History: Surrey.*

POULTON, Rob (1988); *Archaeological Investigations on the site of Chertsey Abbey*; Surrey Archaeological Society; Research volume no.11.

POULTON, Rob (1990); *Saxon Secrets in Surrey;* Esso, Leatherhead.

STEVENS, P.J. (1994); *Surrey Heath in the Dark Ages;* Surrey Heath Local History Club.

Wildlife

LEVER, C. (1977); *The Naturalised Animals of the British Isles*; Hutchinson.

LOCKWOOD, W. B. (1984); *The Oxford Book of British Bird Names;* OUP.

YALDEN, Derek (1999); *The History of British Mammals*; T & A D Poysner Natural History.

Woad

ACKNOWLEDGEMENTS

I would like to express my appreciation to all those people who have nurtured my interest in the Saxons over the years; it is impossible to list them all. However, in preparing and checking portions of the book text I am indebted to Stuart Adams (research), Sonia Carroll (dogs), Grace Corne (sheep; cereals), L. Gilbert (Judaism), Penny Hollow (birds), Vanessa Jones (moon planting), Kerry Long (Norfolk Horn Sheep), Barry North (Christianity), Brian Rich (place-names and landscape), Jenny Roberts (horses), John Worsfold (sheep), plus the officers at the Weald and Downland Museum, West Stow Anglo-Saxon Village, Museum of London and the RSPB. Thanks are due also to Andrew Stroud for taking the pony photographs from which to draw and to Grace Corne for the samples of corn for the photographs. I am especially grateful to Rob Poulton of the Surrey Archaeological Unit for his support of the project and for reviewing much of the archaeological content for Surrey. His comments and recommendations were invaluable and so were those of Gordon Weaver who undertook the proof reading of the text. Finally, I am indebted to Aaron Mason for converting my text, illustrations and design ideas into the book and especially for his goodwill and patience when I continually asked for adjustments. Thank you all very much.

INDEX

Abstract qualities listed as cultural traits, and, aspects of growing up as rites of passage.

Only footnotes with significant extra detail indexed.

Selected illustrations indexed in bold.